200 Quilting tips, techniques & trade secrets

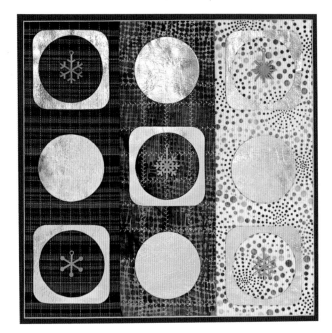

200 Quilting tips, techniques & trade secrets

Susan Briscoe

St. Martin's Griffin
New York

200 QUILTING TIPS, TECHNIQUES &
TRADE SECRETS. Copyright © 2008
by Quarto Inc. All rights reserved.
Printed in China. For information,
address St. Martin's Press,
175 Fifth Avenue, New York,
N.Y. 10010.

www.stmartins.com

Library of Congress Cataloging-in-
Publication Data Available Upon Request

ISBN-13: 978-0-312-38862-1
ISBN-10: 0-312-38862-4

First St. Martin's Press Edition:
February 2009

QUAR: QTS

Conceived, designed, and produced by
Quarto Publishing
The Old Brewery
6 Blundell Street
London N7 9BH

Senior editor: Katie Hallam
Co-editor: Ruth Patrick
Copy editor: Liz Dalby
Art director: Caroline Guest
Managing art editor: Anna Plucinska
Art editor: Jackie Palmer
Designer: Julie Francis
Photographers: Karl Adamson and
    Simon Pask
Picture research: Sarah Bell

Creative Director: Moira Clinch
Publisher: Paul Carslake

Manufactured by SC(Sang Choy)
    International Pte Ltd., Singapore
Printed in China by 1010 Printing
    International Limited

10 9 8 7 6 5 4 3 2

Contents

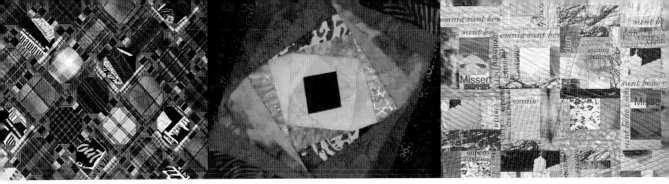

Introduction

Whether you are new to the craft of patchwork and quilting or are already an enthusiast, this book will help you through the process of creating your next project from start to finish. It contains a wealth of technical knowhow and handy tips in the form of easy-to-follow articles to help you achieve the most from your patchwork and quilting. There are over 200 professional fixes, insider tips, and secrets arranged by topic—all the information you need to achieve a great quilt. It includes plenty of those little tricks that really make the difference—the essential quilter's trade secrets!

Patchwork and quilting designs range from the very simple to the more complex, so there's something for every level of ability whether you like traditional, contemporary, or "art" quilt styles. Each topic is fully explained and illustrated with step-by-step photographs, including work by prizewinning quilters, and detailed illustrations. For ease of use, topics are cross-referenced, so you can dip in and out for help and advice, and are arranged in a logical sequence, from choosing your equipment and materials to finishing the quilt. This book will be a much used addition to any quilter's library.

If you want to know how to select the best fabrics to show off your patchwork design, rotary cut with safety and accuracy, achieve the "wow" factor with exciting color choices, sew a true quarter-inch seam, and many more aspects of this fascinating craft—while, most importantly, enjoying creating unique quilts—this is the book for you.

Susan Briscoe

About this book

Aimed at quilters of all levels, this book shares over 400 expert fixes, tips, and insider secrets that will enable any crafter to achieve great results every time. The information is organized by topic and includes clear instructions and helpful photography.

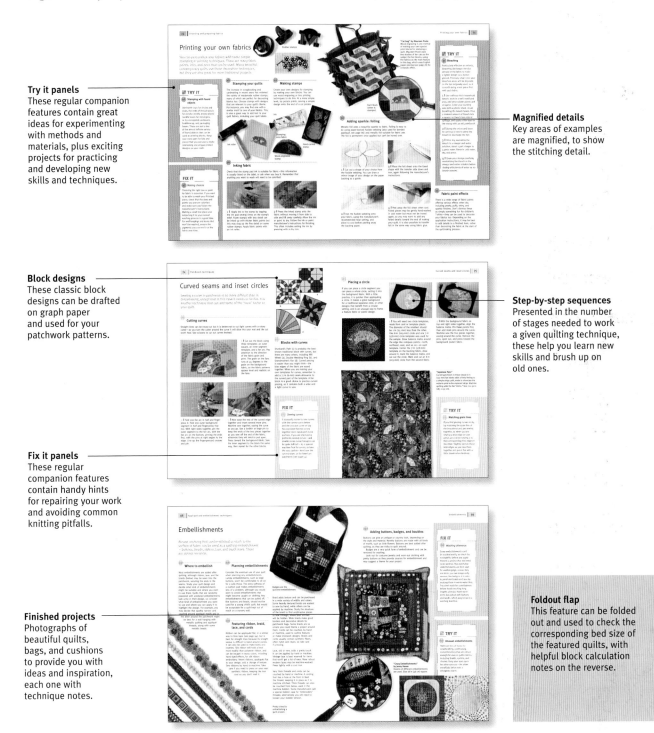

Try it panels
These regular companion features contain great ideas for experimenting with methods and materials, plus exciting projects for practicing and developing new skills and techniques.

Magnified details
Key areas of examples are magnified, to show the stitching detail.

Block designs
These classic block designs can be drafted on graph paper and used for your patchwork patterns.

Step-by-step sequences
Presented in the number of stages needed to work a given quilting technique, these help you learn new skills and brush up on old ones.

Fix it panels
These regular companion features contain handy hints for repairing your work and avoiding common knitting pitfalls.

Finished projects
Photographs of beautiful quilts, bags, and cushions to provide you with ideas and inspiration, each one with technique notes.

Foldout flap
This feature can be folded out and used to check the corresponding bed size of the featured quilts, with helpful block calculation notes on the reverse.

CHOOSING EQUIPMENT

Having the right tools on hand will help your quiltmaking be a pleasurable activity and will enable you to take full advantage of modern technology while crafting beautiful quilts.

What you really need

You may already have the equipment on the following pages in your everyday sewing basket—if not, you can buy a wide variety of quilting equipment from your local quilting store or craft store, by mail order, or over the Internet (see Useful addresses, page 153). Buy the best equipment you can afford and it will last for years.

Hand sewing needles

Fabric scissors

Embroidery scissors

1 Scissors

Use fabric scissors for cutting fabric, embroidery scissors for cutting threads, and paper scissors for rough-cutting paper-backed fusible webbing—don't blunt your fabric scissors by using them to cut paper. A pair of thread snips are also handy for snipping threads at the machine.

2 Needles for hand sewing

"Sharps" are useful for basting layers before quilting—buy a selection of sizes. "Betweens" can be used for hand quilting, or use smaller sharps. A "crewel" embroidery needle is good for finishing off loose appliqué threads; the longer eye makes it easy to thread. Keep a needlethreader handy if you have problems threading needles. Look out for special sharps with slightly larger eyes for the needle size, such as no. 9 sharps with no. 10 eyes. Select a needle that will pass through your fabric easily, but is large enough for the thread you are using—pulling a thick thread through fabric with too small a needle is hard work and will make your wrists ache.

3 Needles for machine sewing

"Universal" needles in sizes 10–12 (US) or 70–80 (Europe) are fine for machine piecing, but you will get a better result with a Microtex needle, especially for finer fabrics such as silk. The point of a universal needle tends to push the fabric threads apart, while a Microtex needle pierces the fabric. "Quilting" needles are very sharp, designed to stitch through batting and fabric layers, and are best for machine quilting. Use "embroidery" needles for machine embroidery threads and "metallica" or "heavy metal" needles for metallic embroidery threads. Their eyes are larger and less prone to wearing and snagging these specialist threads.

Machine sewing needles

Safety pins

Flower pins

Fine pins

4 Pins and safety pins

Select fine pins, such as good-quality dressmaking pins or "silk" pins, for piecing patchwork. "Flower" pins have a flat head so they don't twist on the fabric. Safety pins can be used to hold the layers together for quilting, instead of basting—curved quilter's safety pins are easier for this. If you need to leave pins in your work for any length of time, check that they are rustproof.

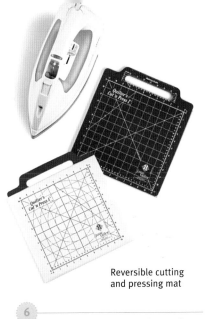

Reversible cutting
and pressing mat

5

Threads for machine and hand sewing

50s (medium thickness) cotton sewing thread is best for piecing. Using thicker thread will bulk up patchwork seams and reduce the accuracy of your piecing.

Choose a neutral color that blends with your fabrics. Grays, browns, and dull khaki greens are surprisingly useful. Use 30s or 40s (thicker) cotton sewing thread for machine or hand quilting. Special quilting threads include variegated thread, which may blend in better when you are quilting large-patterned fabrics.

Hand quilting threads are treated to allow for smooth hand sewing. They have a slight springiness that helps resist accidental knotting but means they are unsuitable for machine sewing. Other threads are treated with beeswax or silicone wax to resist knotting—pull the thread over the edge of the wax block several times.

Hand quilting
threads

Thread for piecing
patchwork

6

Iron and ironing board

An ordinary iron and ironing board are ideal for pressing blocks. If your fabric doesn't press easily with a dry iron, try a shot of steam, but avoid steaming blocks excessively as this can distort the patchwork. Steam-pressing finished blocks or quilt-tops is fine. A small travel iron or a mini-appliqué iron is best for ironing on bias tape. A pressing mat or small ironing board is convenient to use near your sewing machine, although having your ironing station set up in another room will encourage you to move around more when you sew!

7

Rotary cutter

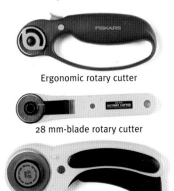

Ergonomic rotary cutter

28 mm-blade rotary cutter

45 mm-blade "squeeze release" cutter

A rotary cutter with a 28-mm or 45-mm blade will be most useful (blades are sold in metric sizes only). Try out several cutters to find one with the handle shape and blade guard that suits your hand best. The blades are razor-sharp, so always replace the blade guard after cutting and never leave the cutter where children or pets can reach it. Check you can operate the blade guard easily—the older style of cutter has a sliding guard, but cutters with "squeeze-release" guards might be easier for you. The cutter must be used with a mat. Keep old, dull blades for cutting paper, if you also enjoy paper crafts.

8

Ruler

A rectangular ruler approximately 14 in (350 mm) long and 4½ in (114 mm) wide with 60-degree and 45-degree markings is ideal. A square ruler is useful for squaring up finished blocks. Look at the line markings and choose colors you will be able to see against your fabric. Buy the same make of ruler consistently, as measurements can vary slightly between manufacturers. Use a tape measure to measure across the quilt to add borders or binding, and measure curves with the tape on its edge.

Square and rectangular
quilting rulers

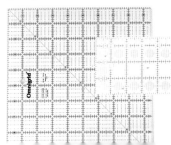

9

Cutting mat

A large cutting mat is best—18 x 24 in (approximately A2) is a good size. Smaller mats can make cutting difficult if you need to keep fat quarters flat (without folding), but are useful for taking to classes. Choose a mat with a printed grid, either imperial or metric depending which you prefer. Store your mat flat and away from heat and sunlight, which will melt and warp it—if this happens, soften your mat in a bath of warm water and allow it to cool with weights to press it flat. Check that the measurements are still accurate afterward! Mats that are no longer in good enough condition for patchwork are useful for other crafts, but don't spoil your patchwork mat by cutting on it with craft knives.

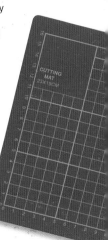

Your sewing machine

Unless you intend to dedicate your patchwork and quilting to hand work only, you will need a sewing machine. It is the most substantial single sewing investment you will make, so choose carefully!

10 Buying a machine

Several manufacturers produce machines aimed at the quilting enthusiast with all the features you will need. Visit a store to try out various machines. Sellers have sales stands at national quilting and textile shows, where you can "test drive" their machines—there are often big discounts at shows, too. Check that the seller offers a good back-up service. Some stores include basic tuition or free machining lessons with purchase—great for beginners.

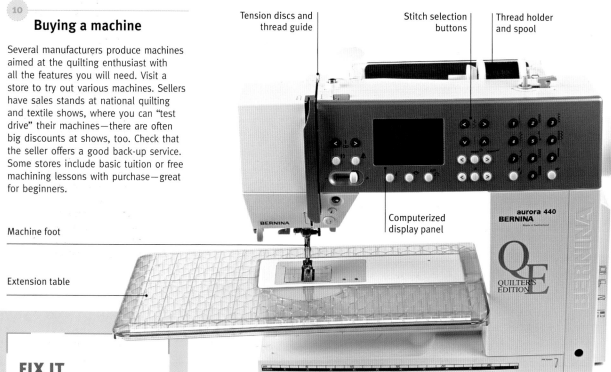

Tension discs and thread guide

Stitch selection buttons

Thread holder and spool

Machine foot

Computerized display panel

aurora 440
BERNINA
Made in Switzerland

Extension table

FIX IT

11 *Maintenance*

Read the manual and try out all the relevant features. Simple mistakes—like wrongly threading a new machine's bobbin mechanism in the same way as your old one—can cause problems. If you have bought a reconditioned machine or have lost the manual, you can download replacements for many machines from the Internet—type your machine's name and number into the search engine—or contact the manufacturer. Think of your machine like a car and keep it adequately maintained for years of happy sewing mileage.

12 Secondhand machines

You may have the chance to buy an excellent secondhand machine, from a private seller or a store. If you know the make and model you want and are experienced with sewing machines, this option can save on cost. A store will have reconditioned the machine and will probably offer a short warranty; ask a private seller to have a service done for you. There is no point buying a machine that doesn't work properly or doesn't do what you need. Some vintage machine models, such as the Singer Featherweight series, are collectible and the price will reflect this.

13 Moving your machine

The machine should be sturdy and stable, but not too heavy. If you sew on the dining table and have to put your machine away when it is not in use, a heavy machine will discourage you from setting up your workspace. It is also a problem if you plan to attend workshops. Even if you invest in a cushioned sewing machine trolley, you will still need to set up your machine in class. Pack your machine carefully for workshops and place it in your car's footwell or strapped to the backseat—it will get jolted and damaged in the trunk.

14

Check the stitch options

Look for a well-designed stitch function layout on the machine, where you can easily find the stitches you will use most and change between them. You don't need lots of stitches, but a good straight stitch is a must, and a good zigzag is also necessary if you want to sew satin-stitch-edged machine appliqué. Machine blanket stitch is also suitable for appliqué. Features such as machine buttonholes, a zipper foot, and an overlock stitch might not seem relevant to patchwork but are handy for finishing items like cushions or bags.

15

Patchwork and quilting features

For patchwork, a "needle-down" option—so the machine can be set to stop with the needle in the down position—helps with sewing longer sections together. It is essential for free-motion machine quilting with an embroidery foot (see page 87), as the foot will not hold the fabric in place when you stop sewing if the needle is in the "up" position.

Quarter-inch foot

A ¼-in (6-mm) foot will help you to sew an accurate ¼-in (6-mm) seam, the standard patchwork seam. The standard machine foot is slightly wider than this—approximately ⁵⁄₁₆ in (7.5-mm), so, even with a ¼-in (6-mm) guide on your machine sole-plate, it will be difficult to maintain an accurate seam. Your patchwork pieces won't fit together if your seam allowances are larger or smaller than ¼ in (6 mm), if that is the seam allowance you have cut.

Walking foot

For machine quilting straight lines and gentle curves, a walking foot is essential. It feeds the top fabric and batting through at the same rate that the machine's feed dogs are feeding the backing through, so the quilt's layers aren't pushed out of alignment as you stitch. Because the walking foot synchronizes with your machine feed, you must have the correct foot for your machine model. A cut away "toe" at the front of the foot enables you to see your sewing clearly—a must when quilting "in the ditch" (along the seam line).

Embroidery foot

"Free motion" machine quilting uses an embroidery, or quilting, foot which moves up and down with the needle, allowing you to move the fabric in any direction you wish. To do this, the feed dogs must be set in the "down" position, so they don't try to pull the fabric through the machine. Most modern machines will have this feature.

17

Other features

Many modern machines have a free arm for dressmaking, and an extension table can be slotted onto the machine to give a level area for patchwork and quilting. Larger extension tables are available for all machines to make machine quilting easier, as the quilt is more evenly supported. Top-of-the-range computerized machines now include a stitch-length sensor that regulates the stitch length so your stitching is even.

▪ TRY IT

16 Really straight stitching

Most modern machines can stitch straight or zigzag stitches. However, you may notice that the straight stitch has a slight waviness, as the needle moves from side to side slightly through the slot in the throat-plate even when the machine is set to straight stitching. This slot also causes problems with free-motion machine quilting, as the needle can be dragged sideways and spoil your quilting. The answer is to buy a straight-stitch throat plate, with a hole rather than a slot, and use this for straight stitching only. Your machine will sew straighter and there's no chance of dragging the stitch line in free motion. Remember to replace the original plate when you want to zigzag though, or you'll shatter the needle!

Zigzag throat plate

Straight-stitch throat plate

Quilting gadgets

In addition to the basics mentioned on pages 10–11, there are many handy bits and pieces designed for the modern quilter—here's a sample of the best. You will find some more useful than others, but it is certainly worth checking out anything new when visiting a quilting store or show, or if you're browsing a catalog or website.

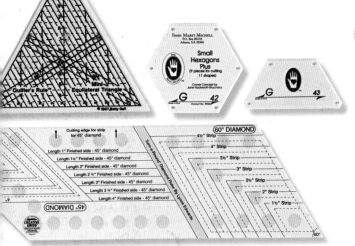

Triangular ruler, hexagon templates, and diamond ruler

18 Rulers and templates

If you are planning a large project or several items using a particular patchwork design, specialist rulers and templates can speed up your cutting out. As well as the usual rectangular and square quilters' rulers, there are rulers to help you cut 60-degree diamond patterns such as Lone Star, wedge rulers for patterns such as Dresden Plate, and simplified rulers for Log Cabin strips (see page 57). There are also rulers to help you cut tricky designs accurately: Drunkard's Path curved segments (see page 74) or Lantern blocks, for example. Like rulers, they are made from acrylic, with clear markings and non-slip backings. Template sets for particular designs are also available. The more specific a ruler or template set, the less useful it will be in general terms, but it will be invaluable for cutting that particular pattern.

19 Marking your fabric

Drawing easy-to-see yet easy-to-remove light lines on dark fabrics used to be a problem, but a white rollerball marking pen is easier to use than a hard white pencil and the marks come out easily. Use a blue wash-out marking pen for light fabrics. Apply and remove any pen marks according to the manufacturer's instructions. Chemical markers must be washed out, not simply left to fade away, as residue could rot your fabric. If your project isn't going to be washed, use pencils or chalk to mark your patterns, embroidery motifs, or appliqué outlines.

Marking pencils

Marking pens

Brass disk

A $\frac{1}{2}$-in (13-mm) diameter brass disk can be used to add a $\frac{1}{4}$-in (6-mm) seam allowance to any template. With the point of a pencil in the center hole and the edge against the template, trace around the template—a $\frac{1}{4}$-in (6-mm) seam allowance will be added to the shape all around. This is useful for curved templates.

Point turner

A point turner, in either bamboo or plastic, is kinder than the point of your scissors when turning corners right-side out—use it for the corners of cushions or when "bagging out" quilted items and finishing the edges without binding.

Point turner

TRY IT

20 Using a ruby viewer

Viewing your fabrics through a red-tinted piece of plastic or cellophane helps you to evaluate the tones of your fabric without being distracted by the colors. Use a candy wrapper or invest in a ruby viewer. It works for all colors except reds, as the fabrics will appear as shades of red when viewed.

Bias tape

Bias tape is used for certain appliqué designs, including Celtic-style appliqué. Readymade bias tape with a fusible adhesive strip makes this appliqué even easier and with a bias tape maker, you can make the tape from coordinating fabric and apply the adhesive strip to the back too.

Thimbles

Get nimble with your thimble! There are many different kinds of thimbles made especially for quilters, so even if you don't like the traditional rigid metal thimble, you may find you get along well with a leather or plastic thimble. Try out several until you find the one that suits your fingers best, and make sure it fits correctly. It will save your fingers when hand quilting in a frame or hoop, when you will also need a thimble on your left hand (see hand quilting, page 110).

Mini-iron

A mini-iron is great for fused appliqué, applying fusible bias tape and other applications where you need heat in a very small area. Its tiny point saves toasting your fingers with a full-size iron.

Seam ripper

When disaster strikes and you sew something you didn't want to sew, you will be glad of your seam ripper. Use it to carefully cut every other stitch and tease out the threads.

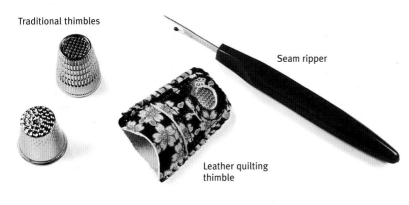

Traditional thimbles

Seam ripper

Leather quilting thimble

¼-in (6-mm) seam disk

Graph paper

Graph paper or squared paper is invaluable as a quilt planning aid. Use it to quickly sketch out ideas for quilts, allocating a unit, such as 1-in (25-mm) or 2-in (50-mm) squares, so you can easily work out sizes of finished patchwork pieces. Isometric graph paper has an equilateral triangle grid, perfect for patterns requiring 60-degree angles. Both square and isometric graph papers are specially made for quilters with ¼-in (6-mm) increments, so you can use them to make paper templates too.

FIX IT

21 *Coating threads*

Threads made for machine use (most modern threads) will twist and knot as you sew and may need some encouragement to make them behave when you are hand sewing. Coating the thread with beeswax or silicone wax will help prevent knots and the thread will slip through your fabric more easily. Run the thread over a beeswax block, pressing it against the surface with your thumb, then smooth the wax by running the thread through your fingers. Sandwich the threads between two sheets of absorbent kitchen paper or cloth and press them with a hot iron to make the threads absorb the wax. Some hand quilters like to prepare up to 20 threads this way at the start of each quilting session. Silicone-coated threads come ready to use.

Silicone wax block

CHOOSING AND PREPARING FABRICS

From reproduction vintage prints to the most modern designs, today's quilter has access to thousands of gorgeous fabrics to inspire their work. Give your quilts a boost by making sure you select the best possible fabric.

Selecting patchwork cottons

There are patchwork fabrics to suit all tastes and styles. Choose 100 percent cotton fabric—polycottons are not suitable for quilting—and buy the best you can afford. Quilting cotton is sometimes called "dress-weight" cotton. It holds a crease when pressed, so is easy for beginners to use.

◼ TRY IT

22 Adding new fabric

If you run out of fabric in a project, try adding another that is similar in tone and pattern, rather than rushing out to buy more of the same. It will add interest to your quilt!

◼ TRY IT

23 Adding movement

Directional fabrics, including printed stripes and checks, can add dynamic movement to a quilt. Take care to cut your pieces so the pattern runs the way you want.

• **Plain cottons** are dyed after weaving and are produced in dozens of colors. They will show off your quilting designs clearly.

• **Shot cottons** are woven with different colors for the warp and weft. They have subtle color accents and will show your quilting well.

• **Striped cottons**, woven or printed, add structure and a sense of movement to your patchwork. You can follow the lines in your quilting.

• **Checked cottons** can be woven or printed. They will add a sense of movement when used on the diagonal or calm the design when used straight.

• **Printed spots and dots** can be lively or subtle, depending on the color contrast and size of the dots. They are best combined with other prints, as too many dots can be overwhelming.

• **Small or mini-prints** disguise patchwork seams and camouflage quilting stitches.

Plains, weaves, and prints from different ranges can be coordinated.

Coordinated prints
from the same range.

• **Cotton flannel** is brushed for a soft appearance and is perfect for country-style quilts.

• **Metallic cottons** have printed highlights that add sparkle, usually on top of a printed or dyed design.

• **Large prints or feature fabrics** give lots of pattern variety and are good for "fussy cutting" (see page 50).

• **Directional prints** have motifs arranged in stripes or have an obvious right way up.

• **Tone-on-tone prints** are useful as a calming alternative to plains and as a transition between patterns.

• **Batiks and hand-dyes** are often colorful but can also be subtle, with shaded color changes across the fabric.

• **Ombre fabrics** have shaded effects, changing color or tone from side to side or along their length. They may be woven, printed, or hand-dyed.

24 Buying quilting fabric

When choosing your fabrics, consider whom you are making the quilt for—bright colors might be great for a child's quilt, but you might prefer something more subdued for yourself.

• If you are aiming for a particular style, such as 1930s or Amish, look for fabrics that will suit the design.
• Many stores sell patchwork fabric as "fat quarters" (a yard or meter quartered into roughly square pieces), "thin quarters" (a linear quarter yard or meter), "half" yards or meters, and by the yard. If you think you will use a lot of a fabric, consider buying two yards, but for accent fabric, a fat quarter will probably be enough. See page 152 for calculating fabric quantities.
• Buying fabrics as fat quarter bundles means the job of coordinating colors and patterns has been done for you!
• If you anticipate needing more fabric, keep the printed selvedge strips as a reference, so you can identify the fabric and colorway.
• Look out for sales, which are a good time to stock up on fabrics for quilt backings at reduced prices. Your backing fabric needs to be similar quality to your quilt top—polycotton sheeting will not make a nice backing and will be difficult to hand quilt, as the weave is too tight.
• New patchwork fabric collections can turn over almost as quickly as high street fashions, so don't expect ranges to be in stock for years on end. Be prepared to search further afield for out-of-print (OOP) fabrics.
• You don't need to be 100 percent in love with every fabric in your quilt, but if you hate the fabric from the outset, you probably won't enjoy working with it.
• Avoid cheap, low-quality fabrics—they can be rough to work with, may fray or fade easily, and won't wear well.
• Don't forget mail order and the Internet; both excellent sources of patchwork fabric. The world is your oyster—or your fabric source, anyway!

• **Feature panels** (also called "cheater panels") have landscapes and large designs. Popular for pictorial cushion panels, they can be incorporated into patchwork with interesting effects.

Special fabrics

You can use fabrics other than cotton for patchwork and quilting. Many vintage quilts were made with silks and velvets, while art quilters use all kinds of fabrics, including synthetics, to achieve special effects—there have even been quilts made from plastic bags. Since most of these fabrics can't be washed, you may want to use them for a wall hanging rather than a sofa throw.

■ TRY IT

25 Using one color

Using a single color in an assortment of fibers and fabrics can make for interesting and unusual contrasts in your quilt. As the fabrics reflect light in different ways, the same color will appear lighter and darker. This technique is also good for quilts in natural, unbleached fabrics, such as undyed silks and linens.

FIX IT

26 *Preventing fraying*

Silks, linens, and some wools fray more readily than cotton patchwork fabrics. Looser weaves will tend to fray too. Very fine fabrics can be backed with a lightweight iron-on interfacing to help control fraying. You may need to use larger seam allowances than the normal $\frac{1}{4}$-in (6 mm). Thicker wools are better for techniques like raw edge appliqué than patchwork, backed with iron-on interfacing first.

• **Velvet** is very tactile and is made from cotton, silk, or man-made fibers. Depending on the fiber used, the pile may look matte or glossy. Crushed velvet reflects light and looks shiny. Cotton velvet is thick, so you may prefer to try thinner cotton velveteen for a similar effect. The pile threads are messy when cut, so be prepared to keep cleaning up your workspace and machine.

• **Silk** adds shine to a quilt. It is available in many weaves and weights. Slubbed dupion is most popular for quilts. Satin weaves highlight quilted detail. Japanese kimono silk and Indian silks give an exotic look. Thin silks and stretchy silks, like crêpe, are best backed with iron-on stabilizer if you want to use them for piecing. Thin silk gauze is good for shadow quilting.

• **Wool** is produced in many different weaves and thicknesses, in both smooth and rough textures. Preshrink wools by steam-pressing before you start cutting out, otherwise they may shrink when you press your work later on.

• **Sheer fabrics** in various fibers are great for layering effects, such as shadow quilting (see page 97). Some have metallic threads in the weave.

• **Lace** is great for crazy patchwork (see page 100) and other projects that require embellishment (see page 98). Lace fabrics will need to be layered over another fabric to prevent batting coming through the holes.

• **Cotton sateen** has a subtle sheen. It is perfect for emphasizing quilting contours and is the traditional material for British wholecloth quilts.

• **Man-made fibers** are not easy to use for traditional patchwork, as they don't crease easily and can be slippery to sew; but they are good for special effects on contemporary quilts. Sheer nylon gauze can be layered or used as the top fabric for shadow quilting.

Velvet, silk, and vintage cotton print

Lace
and net

Nylon gauze

Bleached velvet

• **Linen** adds an interesting matte texture and gives a country-style look.

• **Exotics** such as Japanese silks, ikats, African tie-dyes, wax batiks, and Indian sari fabrics will give your quilts a different style. Where appropriate, prewash cottons, as they are likely to bleed dye, and be careful of combining them with pale fabrics if you want to make a washable quilt.

• **Furnishing fabrics** are generally too thick to use for conventional patchwork piecing, but lighter curtain fabrics and some textured weaves can be used for innovative appliqué techniques or for parts of patchwork bags and cushions.

• **Vintage fabrics** can be used to add unique accents. They are likely to be weaker than new fabrics, so treat them carefully—perhaps reserving them for heirloom projects. Patchwork combining weaker vintage fabrics with new materials is likely to put considerable strain on the older pieces along the seam lines and is not recommended.

Experiment
with color
and texture.

Preparing and storing fabrics

Before you begin work, it is a good idea to prewash cotton fabrics for any project that you will want to wash later on, such as bed quilts, cushions, bags, table decorations, and children's items.

FIX IT

27 *Preventing unraveling*

Snip a tiny triangle from the corner of each fabric piece before washing, to keep the warp threads from unraveling. For more loosely woven cottons like brushed flannel, zigzag the edges before washing to prevent unraveling.

▦ TRY IT

28 Adding starch

Once your fabrics are washed and ready to press, they will feel a bit limp, as all the starchy finish will have been washed out of them. Replace this by spray-starching your fabrics before pressing them dry. Pale-colored fabrics can be starched by adding a liquid starch to the rinse cycle, but these tend to leave light streaks on darker fabrics. Putting the crispness back into your fabric will make it easier to work with, and the starchy feeling will disappear with use. If you live in a part of the world where starched fabrics tend to attract bugs, dry your fabrics and starch them just before use, washing the starch out of the finished item later.

29
An initial wash

A quick machine wash will flush out any excess dye and preshrink the fabric. Sort your fabrics into groups of similar colors first and open pieces out. Loosely fill the machine, so the fabrics won't rub together too much in the wash. Put a dye-grabbing or color-catching cloth (sold in grocery stores' laundry sections) in with the fabrics to catch any loose dye. Use a gentle detergent without optical brighteners. Wash the fabrics using the same temperature cycle you would use for the finished item—a 40-degree cycle is generally fine. Tumble- or line-dry them until they are damp, not bone-dry.

31
Use your scraps

It is all too easy to keep putting your scraps in a box and never do anything with them. Organize by strip width, putting 1-in (25-mm) strips in one box, 1½-in (38-mm) strips in another, and so on, so you have a readymade resource (below). Irregular shapes can go in another box for appliqué and crazy patchwork. Every so often, make a quilt from your scraps, give them away to a quilting friend, bag them up for fundraising sales, or even have a scrap-piecing party.

30
Storage solutions

Quilters build up impressive fabric stashes, which need to be organized. Depending on the quilts you make and the fabrics you like, you can organize your collection in various ways, such as by size and color (sets of fat quarters of different colors), by theme and pattern (oriental, country, 1930s), by tone (lights, darks, and medium tones), or by type (flannels, woven stripes, batiks).

Choose a system that works for you. If you want to make scrap quilts that rely on tonal changes, a basket of light tones and another of darks may be all you need. You might purchase fabrics with a particular project in mind, keeping all the pieces together until you begin. Plastic boxes, tubs, and baskets are good for storing fabrics, with your fat quarters and half yards folded, like in a quilt store. Check out underbed storage (plastic or canvas), canvas hanging storage for wardrobes, and plastic drawer units among household goods ranges. Make sure air can circulate in lidded plastic boxes to prevent mold. Larger fabric pieces can be hung from clothes hangers in a wardrobe. Keep your fabrics out of direct sunlight to prevent fading.

32
Straightening the grain line

Sometimes fabrics are slightly off-grain as they have become stretched and distorted along the edges by being wound onto the bolt. Checks and stripes are particularly prone to this problem. You can gently pull the fabric square again as you press and hold it square by starching. Don't do this for techniques like Stack-n-Whack® (page 51), where it is important that the fabric pattern should match up as printed.

Dyeing your own fabrics

When you can't find the fabric you want, why not dye it yourself? Popular with contemporary and art quilters, many different effects are possible with this technique, from subtly tinting the fabric, to changing the color all over, to bright tie-dyed and shibori effects. Fabric dyes for natural fibers are easy to buy and easy to use, as long as you follow some basic safety rules.

■ TRY IT

33 Using dyes safely

Dyes and the chemicals used to fix them into the fibers are toxic. Always follow the manufacturer's safety instructions and these general guidelines:
• Do not use food utensils to measure or mix dyes.
• Cover work surfaces with plastic sheeting or, better still, work in an area that is not used for food preparation.
• Clearly label any chemicals and dye solutions that are not in their original bottles—it is easy to mix them up.
• Store dyes, chemicals, and equipment away from pets and children, in a cool, dry place. Don't store them where they might be mistaken for food.
• Wear rubber gloves and an apron, to keep the chemicals off your skin.
• Wear a face mask and don't inhale dye powders; work in a well ventilated area.
• Wash splashes off immediately with soap and water; mop up any spills straight away.
• Don't eat, drink, or smoke while working with dyes.
• Dispose of any dye residues and leftovers down the drain, with plenty of running water to dilute them. If you have septic tank drainage, you will need to bottle up the residue and take it to a suitable disposal point.

34 Dyeing equipment

You will need only basic equipment, including buckets for dyeing and rinsing, trays and containers for dyeing, a measuring jug, measuring spoons, and protective covering for your work area and clothes. Keep dyeing equipment and cooking equipment separate.

36 Fiber-reactive dyes

Procion MX is a cold water fiber-reactive dye. It needs to be mixed with salt, urea, and soda ash or washing soda. The fabric needs immersing in the dye bath for 15 minutes before a solution of soda ash is added, then remains in the dye for a further hour. Use a specialist detergent to rinse out excess dye afterward (check with your dye supplier for a suitable brand). Very vivid, saturated colors are possible.

38 Cold water dyes

Cold water dyes normally require a fixative and extra salt, and are dissolved in hot water, before adding cold water to the dye bath. The fabric needs to be in the dye bath for an hour, before being rinsed and washed in a normal detergent. Cold water dye colors tend to be more subdued than machine dyes.

35 Store-bought dyes

Make sure you get instructions for the dyeing process when you buy your dye. Dyes sold in grocery stores, drugstores, and DIY stores usually have instructions on the packaging, but some dyes sold in art stores and fabric stores may require an instruction leaflet. If in doubt, ask. Prewash fabrics to remove any stain-resistant finishes and starches, and leave them damp to absorb the dye.

37 Machine dyes

Machine dyes are formulated to dye natural fibers on a 60-degree wash cycle, and excess dye is flushed out of the machine by running a hot wash cycle straight after the fabric is dyed, using a normal detergent. They usually require extra salt, although some packs are sold with the salt mixed in. Colors are quite strong and bright on cotton. They can be used for hand dyeing too.

Japanese indigo shibori

40 Using microwave dyes

Some machine dyes can be used in the microwave (check the packaging for suitability before trying this method). This is excellent for tie-dyed and blotchy dye effects, as the fabric is in the dye for only four minutes and has only a short time to penetrate the fibers. Mix a small batch of dye in a microwave-safe glass dish and arrange your fabrics in it. Use the confined space to immerse some parts of the fabric bundles in the dye, while keeping others out of the dye. Put a lid on the dish and microwave on high for four minutes. The dish will be very hot once the dye is cooked, so take care handling it. Rinse and finish the fabric as usual.

39 Anyone for tea?

Dyeing fabric with tea tones down the colors and gives an antique effect. Jasmine tea gives an attractive creamy-yellow tone, while blended teas tend to give a pinkish color. With boiling water, brew up a strong mixture of tea in a bowl, using slightly more tea than you would if you intended to drink it. Use teabags rather than loose tea so the leaves don't stick to your fabric. Once the tea is a dark color, take out the teabags and add the fabric. Leave the fabric in the tea until it is a shade or two darker than the desired color, as it will lose some of the color when rinsed. The process can be speeded up by cooking the fabric in the tea for four minutes in a microwave on maximum power. Tea-dyed fabrics tend to darken with time, so don't overdo the dyeing.

Soften black and white prints by tea-dyeing.

41 Indigo dyeing

Natural indigo dyeing can be done at home with a dye kit but it is a smelly process, requiring caustic soda and other chemicals. Follow the instructions supplied with the kit carefully. The dye bath needs to be kept at a constant temperature and the cloth should be removed from the dye bath with great care, pulling it out slowly and away from the bucket, so the dye doesn't drip back in, oxidizing the dye bath and reducing its effectiveness. The fabric will look pale green initially but the rich blue color will develop as the indigo oxidizes in the atmosphere.

Microwave-dyed greens

42 Shaded effects

Dye your own shaded fabrics (see shaded muslin, below, and background, opposite) by immersing the fabric in the dye bath in sections. Thoroughly dampen the fabric for more even shading. To shade from a dark to a very light color, gradually immerse more of the cloth into the dye, draping the excess over the side of a bucket. Alternatively, try pulling the fabric out of the bucket in stages—you will need another container to hold the dyed fabric as it comes out.

■ TRY IT

43 Tie-dyeing

Often called by its Japanese name, shibori, tie-dyeing is a resist method. Fabric may be knotted, twisted, folded, clamped between boards, bound with string or elastic bands, scrunched, or stitched and gathered tightly. All these methods create a resist and keep the dye from penetrating the fibers. Try scrunching up the fabric and tying for a simple splotched design. Shibori is an art in itself and there are dozens of traditional techniques that you can explore.

Shaded muslin

"The Fabled Hare"
A fabric remnant with only the background color printed made a good central panel after it had been tie-dyed in purple and blue. Starting behind the place for the moon appliqué, it was simply bound with elastic bands to make a halo effect and the rest of the fabric was irregularly pleated, before being dyed in the microwave. Border fabrics were overdyed and tie dyed for more variety. Size 72 in (183 cm) square.

Subtle shaded effects

■ TRY IT

44 Harmonizing colors

Overdyeing or tinting a mismatched set of fabrics with a pale rinse of the same color will harmonize the colors, in a similar way to a painter adding a little of one pigment to all the others to achieve a harmonious effect. This technique is very effective when used on clashing plain colors.

FIX IT

45 Overdyeing

If you feel a finished patchwork or even a completed quilt needs some color improvement or coordination, you can overdye the whole piece to add harmony to the colors. Just a light tint will do the trick. You can add some contrasting color with big-stitch quilting (see page 124) or some embellishments afterward if you feel the quilt needs it. Hand dyeing will be better for an unfinished quilt-top, as machine agitation will fray the seam allowances. Depending on your original colors, you can get some stunning results—for example, a blue and yellow quilt overdyed with pink would become purple and orange!

Printing your own fabrics

Rubber stamps

You can personalize your fabrics with some simple stamping or printing techniques. There are many fabric paints, inks, and pens that can be used. Many beautiful contemporary quilts use these decoration techniques, but they are also great for more traditional projects.

TRY IT

46 Stamping with found objects

Use bottle caps for circles and ovals, the ends of thread spools for circular motifs, empty plastic needle boxes for rectangles, or try corrugated cardboard, bubblewrap, and packaging beans. These are just a few of the almost infinite variety of found objects that can be used as printing blocks. Keep your eyes open for bits and pieces that you can use to make interesting and unique printed designs on your cloth.

FIX IT

47 Making choices

Choosing the right dye or paint for fabric is essential. If you want to be able to wash your finished piece, check that the dyes and paints you use are colorfast and make sure you follow the manufacturer's instructions. Making a small test piece and subjecting it to your normal washing process is a good idea. For wallhangings and items that won't be washed, ensure the pigments you use won't rot the fabric over time.

48 Stamping your quilts

The increase in scrapbooking and cardmaking in recent years has widened the variety of readymade rubber stamps, many of which are perfect for decorating fabrics too. Choose stamps with designs that are relevant to your quilt's theme. For instance, you may find one with a similar motif to one of your fabrics. This is also a great way to add text to your quilt fabrics, including your quilt labels.

Ink roller

49 Making stamps

Create your own designs for stamping by making your own blocks. You can use wood engraving or lino printing techniques to do this. At a more simple level, try potato prints, carving a simple design onto the end of a cut potato.

Ink

Stamping onto fabric

Hand-carved stamp

Wood-engraved stamp

50 Inking fabric

Check that the stamp pad ink is suitable for fabric—this information is usually listed on the label, or ask when you buy it. Remember that anything you want to wash will need to be colorfast!

1 | Apply ink to the stamp by tapping the ink pad several times on the stamp's relief. Foam stamps with less detail can be inked up with thicker fabric paints but this may clog up the fine detail on some rubber stamps. Apply fabric paints with an ink roller.

2 | Press the inked stamp onto the fabric without moving it from side to side and lift away carefully. Allow the ink or paint to dry. Follow the ink or paint manufacturer's instructions for finishing. This often includes setting the ink by pressing with a dry iron.

"Cat bag" by Maureen Poole
Wood engraving is one method of making your own special print blocks for stamping a quilt. Maureen Poole used two studies of her cats as the subject for her blocks, using the fabrics as the main feature in this bag, which uses English paper piecing (see page 78) for a mosaic effect.

Each block center is stamped.

52 Adding sparkle: foiling

Metallic foil adds a beautiful sparkle to fabric. Foiling is easy to do using paper-backed fusible webbing (also used for bonded appliqué, see page 86) and metallic foil suitable for fabric use. The foil is permanent once applied but can't be ironed over.

1 | Cut out a shape of your choice from the fusible webbing. You can draw a mirror image of your design on the paper backing as a guide.

3 | Place the foil sheet onto the fused shape with the transfer side down and iron, again following the manufacturer's instructions.

2 | Iron the fusible webbing onto your fabric, using the manufacturer's recommended heat setting, and allow to cool before peeling away the backing paper.

4 | Peel away the foil sheet when cool. Foiled pieces may be gently hand-washed in cool water but must not be ironed again, so you may want to add any foiled details toward the end of making your quilt. It is also possible to transfer foil in the same way using fabric glue.

■ TRY IT

51 Bleaching

Particularly effective on velvets, bleaching discharges the dye already in the fabric to make a lighter design on a darker ground. Precisely what color your bleached areas will be depends on the dye originally used, so it is worth doing a test piece first with each fabric.

1 | Use ordinary thick household bleach, work in a well-ventilated area, and wear rubber gloves and an apron. Cover your working area with a plastic sheet. Avoid breathing the bleach fumes. Pour a minimal amount of bleach into a saucer, so there's less risk of spillage, and apply a thin layer to the stamp with an old paintbrush.

2 | Stamp the velvet and leave for an hour or two to allow the bleach to discharge the dye.

3 | Once dry, neutralize the bleach in a vinegar and water solution, about 1 part vinegar to 4 parts water. Rinse in cold water, dry, and press.

4 | Clean your stamps carefully, neutralizing the bleach in the vinegar and water solution before rinsing with plenty of water so no bleach remains.

53 Fabric paint effects

There is a wide range of fabric paints offering various effects when dry, including pearly, puffy, shiny, and sparkly finishes. Don't dismiss these as simply something fun for children's T-shirts—they can be used to decorate your fabrics too. Depending on the application instructions, it may be best to add details to a finished item, rather than decorating the fabric at the start of the quiltmaking process.

Your photos on fabric

Creating unique fabrics direct from your computer has never been easier and it must be the ultimate method for creating your own fabric prints. Anything that you can print onto paper can now be printed onto fabric just as easily—it's as simple as that! If you are not computer-savvy, ask a friend or relative to help you get started, and have some fun.

Printed images ready to cut out.

FIX IT

 54 *Improving quality*

Your images will look quite dull on fabric when compared with photo paper prints. Do a test print on cheap printer paper first. Use a photo-editing program (such as Photoshop) to improve your image quality before printing. Try increasing contrast, sharpening, or softening parts of the image and increasing color saturation so faces on fabric don't look washed out. When you print, select the "photo" or "best photo" option on your printer menu. If you can select a paper type, try "photo papers" or "card." Experiment to achieve the best results.

TRY IT

 55 **Adding text**

Use the drawing tools in a word processor to add a photo image behind your text, or draw lots of shapes and fill them in with text and images. Some photo-editing programs allow you to add text too. Word-processed text with different fonts can make an interesting fabric design.

56
Putting ink to fabric

Various brands of ready-to-use fabric are available to print on (right). Most result in colorfast images—check the pack before you buy. You will be printing directly onto the fabric without using transfers that clog up the fabric's weave with plastic and make it unpleasant to sew. Finely woven cotton with a high thread count (200) will give the sharpest images. The fabric comes on a paper backing, similar to freezer paper, which helps it to feed through the printer. The fabric is treated with a special chemical that reacts with heat to set the printer ink permanently and make the image colorfast. Colored fabrics will give your image an overall tint, so bear this in mind if you want to use natural fabric or other colors.

57
Setting liquids

You can use liquid products to prepare your own fabric for printing. Following the manufacturer's instructions, your fabric will need to be soaked in the liquid and then dried. You will need to iron a piece of freezer paper onto the back of your fabric. Use a size compatible with your printer; you can buy it in rolls and cut it to fit. Iron it onto the back of the fabric and trim the completed piece to the exact size.

58
Selecting printer ink

Genuine printer inks give better results than generic or refilled cartridges. Consider how you will use the fabric in your work when choosing inks. Pigment ink withstands handling more than dye-based inks, but the latter are brighter and more resistant to fading. Pigment inks would therefore be better for a lap quilt featuring family photos, but dye-based ink would give brighter colors for a wallhanging. If you are buying a new printer for your photos on fabric, check what kind of ink it uses, as you won't be able to switch between ink types.

Fabrics incorporating text are easy to create and add intrigue to the design.

Use text to convey a message. See page 42 for more information about this quilt.

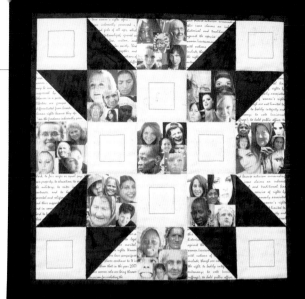

From photo to quilt: image sources

Any digital image can be used, including scanned photos and documents, digital photos, and even word-processed text. Your family photo album, either on disk or on paper, is a good starting point. Don't restrict yourself to views and portraits; capture abstract images and textures as well. If you are scanning photos, check the picture resolution (the "dpi")—it should be 300; you can use a lower resolution to scan a picture if you are using it to scale or smaller. If you plan to enlarge a photo, go for a higher scanning resolution and select the part you wish to use. Scan and work with images in "jpeg" (.jpg) format. Photo-editing software allows you to create negatives, make outlines, and change colors among other features. You can arrange photos on an album page using photo-editing software and print out several photos at once on the same piece of fabric.

Coordinates for digital fabrics

Even the brightest fabrics created on your computer and printed onto fabric at home don't have the intensity of the solid colors you see on commercially screen-printed patchwork fabrics—choose your coordinates with care so they don't make your photo-prints look dull. Batiks and hand-dyed fabrics work well with photo images on fabric, as they have very subtle color changes that are more sympathetic to photographic realism.

"Missenden Now and Then"
Created while the author was Artist in Residence at Missenden Abbey, England, this piece includes images, words, and names from the Abbey's history and its present-day use as a base for residential arts and craft courses. Images were manipulated in various photo-editing and word processing programs, pieced with batik fabric, and machine quilted with hand-dyed threads. Size 42 x 24 in (107 x 61 cm).

Color confidence

You need to make color work for you, to achieve the mood and style you want for your quilt. It is much more exciting to make color discoveries than to simply try to match the bedroom curtains! Use some simple color theory to help you.

TRY IT

61 Selecting a palette

Stumped for your color choices? Coordinate your colors using a favorite postcard or photo for inspiration. Illustrations of favorite paintings are a particularly good source of ideas, as the artist will have already used a selective palette.

62 The color wheel

Colors can be visualized in a circle or "wheel." There is more than one way of dividing up this color wheel. Johannes Itten's color wheel divides colors into 12—the primary, secondary, and tertiary colors—also called "hues."

• **Primary colors** are red, yellow, and blue. They are pure colors—not made by mixing other colors. They are bold and bright.
• **Secondary colors** are orange, green, and violet, made by mixing adjacent primary colors on the color wheel. Yellow and red make orange, yellow and blue make green, and blue and red make violet.
• **Tertiary colors** are made by mixing adjacent primary and secondary colors. For example, red (primary) and orange (secondary) will create red-orange. The tertiaries extend one color into another.

• **Analogous colors** are any three adjacent colors on the wheel, such as blue, blue-violet, and violet. Analogous color combinations have a calm, coordinated, and harmonious effect.
• **Complementary colors** are opposite each other on the color wheel, such as blue and orange. They make each other appear more intense and vivid.
• **Triadic colors** are at the corners of an equilateral triangle overlaid on the wheel—the secondary or tertiary colors as individual groups—such as red, yellow, and blue or orange, green, and violet.
• **Quadratic color** combinations use colors at the corners of a square or rectangle overlaid on the color wheel, such as red-violet, orange, yellow-green, and blue.

"Leafy Satchel"
Shades of green evoke nature, using a secondary color for this monochrome scheme.

"Solstice"
A mostly neutral monochrome fabric selection is warmed up with analogous oranges, reds, and violet. Size 35 x 41 in (89 x 104 cm).

■ TRY IT

63 Inspired by nature

Look at color combinations in nature for inspiration. You will be surprised how many examples of analogous, complementary, triadic, and quadratic colors you can find in plants and flowers. Sometimes quite unexpected and brilliant colors occur quite naturally—use these ideas to plan a quilt color scheme.

64 Talking about color

Colors are further defined by the following terms:
• **Value** describes how light or dark a color appears, from the palest tint to the darkest shade.
• **Tones** are gray mixed with a pure color. As the gray can be light or dark, tones may also be light or dark.
• **Tints** are colors with white added and vary in value depending on how much white is used.
• **Intensity**, or saturation, is used to describe the depth and impact of pure colors.
• **Shades** are colors with black added and vary in value depending on how much black is used.
• **Temperature** describes how warm or cool a color appears. Colors on the red/orange/yellow side of the color wheel are warm, while those on the green/blue/violet side are cool—but yellow with the smallest hint of green will appear cool while violet with a hint of red will appear warm. Cool colors will recede in a design; warm colors will come forward.
• **Monochrome color schemes** are based around tints and tones of a single color—such as blue, white, and all the tints and tones in between—and can also be black and white.
• **Neutrals** include white, black, and grays. They are made by mixing colors from opposite sides of the color wheel. Grays usually have a slight color bias—even completely neutral grays appear to have a hint of color when placed next to a strong hue. Brown, cream, and "natural" undyed or unbleached fabrics also work as neutrals for patchwork.
• **Hue** is simply another word for color.

"Without Hearts or Crosses"
Completely made from 1½-in (38-mm) wide scrap strips, this quilt disregards pattern detail and arranges fabrics by tone, from light to dark and back again. Size 60 in (152 cm) square.

Color creations in practice

Possibilities are explored here with three quilts and three combinations—variations on the theme of analogous colors with contrasting colors, tones, and tints. Each quilt combines a variety of different fabrics—large and small scale patterns, tone-on-tone designs, stripes, and plains.

■ TRY IT

65 Using the dots

Printed fabrics, especially those with lots of colors, usually have a series of dots along the selvedge (below), indicating the individual colors used in the screen printing process. Some of these colors appear in such minute amounts that you will be barely aware of them in the print; others will dominate the design. By using these color dots to coordinate your other fabrics, you are getting a helping hand from the fabric designer! Make sure you include the less obvious colors too to liven up your palette.

66 Plains or patterns?

Solid-color fabrics or "plains" can be tricky to use with patterned fabrics—there tends to be too much contrast and the fabrics don't work well together—so use them with care. A single plain fabric used with a variety of patterns is a traditional option for many quilt designs, but a marbled, spattered, or "tone-on-tone" fabric may achieve a more subtle effect where several colors are needed.

67 Red and yellow rules

Many quilters think that primary red will stand out in a patchwork design—which is true—but primary yellow will really leap out. Deal with these colors by scattering them across a quilt-top, rather than concentrating them in just one area. As a general rule, if a color or fabric stands out too much, add more, not less. The yellow and red fabrics in the "Japanese One of a Kind" sampler quilt are both tone-on-tone fabrics—the mottled yellow is tinted with white and the red is toned down with printed burgundy circles—so the effect isn't overpoweringly bold.

"Japanese One of a Kind"
This teaching sampler combines various techniques. Fabrics were color-coordinated from other fabric ranges using the selvedge dots on the large-scale crane feature fabric, with three light-, dark-, and medium-value prints each, including red and yellow. Size 44 x 38 in (112 x 97 cm).

68 Introducing thread colors

Introduce a subtle touch of color with your quilting thread, either by using a thick thread for big-stitch quilting (see page 124) or by using a 40s or 30s thread for machine or hand quilting (as seen, right, in the thread used to outline the cranes). Even the most vivid colors can be introduced this way without overpowering the fabrics. Don't be discouraged by threads that are ultra colorful and bright on the skein or spool, as they will appear much less intense as a stitched line.

FIX IT

69 *Auditioning fabrics*

Liven up dull color combinations by "auditioning" fabrics in complementary, triadic, or quadratic colors. Take small swatches of your selected fabrics when you go shopping or, even better, take fat quarter pieces so you can get a good impression of how the fabrics will look when used together. If a fabric will only be used in narrow strips, fold and layer it with the other fabrics to give a more accurate impression of how it will look when pieced, as a large area of a vivid color may appear more overpowering than it will once it is cut into smaller pieces and distributed around the quilt-top.

70 Perspective: adding depth

Fabrics that contain a lot of blue or have blurry or small patterns will tend to recede, making objects in a quilt seem farther away. Use this effect to add depth to pictorial quilts. It also works for objects of the same size, such as identical blocks pieced in different colors, say blue and red. If you are making a pictorial quilt, you may want to use the scale of the fabric, as well as the hue and value, to suggest a sense of scale and perspective. Use smaller prints and cooler, darker tones for depth and distance, grading through medium and larger patterns and increasing vibrancy as you come into the foreground.

"Kyoto Dreams"
A triadic combination of red, blue, and yellow, combined with analogous purples, blues, and turquoises, creates depth. The effect is heightened by the darker fabrics used for the inner room and converging lines quilted on the striped "tatami mat" fabric. Size 30 x 20 in (76 x 51 cm).

Tricks with contrast

Become a magician in your use of contrast—you can make patchwork pieces stand out or blend into the background, camouflage seams, and accentuate perspective effects. Mastering contrast in your quilting is just as important as harnessing color effects, whether you want a dramatic or subdued design.

 TRY IT

71 Exploring value

Black and white quilts offer an interesting way to explore value in fabrics, without being distracted by too much color (below). Grade the fabrics by tone, paying attention to the pattern density.

72 Color and value

Some colors inevitably contrast in value—a yellow will be lighter than a red, for example. Combining strong color and value contrasts is an easy way to reveal the patchwork pattern. Less obviously, vibrant effects are created by complementary colors of similar value and intensity. Some quilt styles rely on low color and value contrasts to achieve their distinctive look, such as Japanese taupe quilts, which typically use very low contrasts and gray-toned fabrics. Selecting some fabrics that are darker than required by a block design can also help to emphasize the lighter colors.

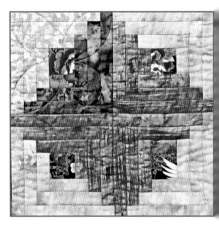

73 Making patterns work: monochromatic contrast

Blocks need sufficient value contrast for the pattern to work. This is particularly important for monochrome quilts. Low contrasting tones, especially if there is also little variation in the color, will make parts of the design seem to disappear.

"Sister's Choice" by Dot Sherlock
Predominantly made from pastel batiks, some of the blocks in this quilt melt into the background while the darker pieces come forward—a reversal of the effect in quilts which are darker overall, where the lighter pieces will seem closer to the viewer. Size 24 in (61 cm) square.

74 Medium-value fabrics

Some fabrics appear light when placed next to the darker fabrics in your palette, while simultaneously appearing dark when placed next to light fabrics. You may therefore be able to use the same fabric as one of your darks in one block and as a light fabric in another. Many traditional blocks require a light, medium, and dark tone, so include these where necessary.

Large-scale prints with light motifs on dark backgrounds (and vice versa) will yield tones and tints when cut for patchwork (right). You may need to evaluate pieces once again after cutting, moving them from the dark tones to the lighter tints range.

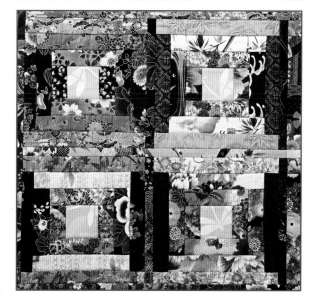

FIX IT

75 Checking values

Check the values of your fabrics by viewing them through a red filter (see page 14). Alternatively try making a black and white scan or photocopy. Arrange the fabrics in order of value from light to dark, as you perceive them, and compare the black and white print. You may be surprised by the results!

"Stash Cupboard Blues" by Rebecca Collins
A limited color palette and controlled use of value in a modern adaptation of the traditional medallion format gives this quilt a calm feeling and a fresh new look to the traditional block designs. Size 72 in (183 cm) square.

76 Tints and tones

Because we inhabit a world lit by a sun from overhead, a "top-down" lighting bias appears natural, while things lit from below tend to look spooky. The same applies to quilts. If the tone of the quilt is darker at the top than the bottom, it will appear top-heavy. To see this effect, try turning this book upside down and viewing "Stash Cupboard Blues" (right) the wrong way up!

Prints and patterns

Large- and small-scale prints, stripes, checks, and other patterns—combine them as you like to create unique effects in your quilt. Allow yourself to use pattern in a creative and intuitive way.

77 Selecting fabric patterns

Cotton patchwork fabrics are usually produced in ranges, which will include feature fabrics (large-scale prints), smaller patterns, and other coordinates; but you can easily coordinate fabric from different manufacturers. Consider the kind of quilt you want to make—for example you will need reproduction 1930s or Civil War fabrics if you want to make a quilt of that era, bright colors if you want to make a quilt with intense bright hues, and so on. You will not be able to achieve the look you want by starting out with the wrong kind of fabric. For example, a selection of bright, novelty fabrics is never going to make a traditional-style quilt that resembles a Victorian hexagon coverlet, and reproduction 1890s fabrics would be entirely inappropriate for a child's I-spy quilt which demands bold images. Some fabrics that are darker than required by a block design can also help to emphasize the lighter colors.

78 Large- and small-scale prints

Unless you are aiming for a particular vintage look, a quilt made entirely of very small prints may feel bland. Even Victorian quilters used a variety of pattern scales, from tiny prints to larger designs, combining geometrics and florals. Mix different scales of design in one project for more interest. Large-scale prints can be cut to provide a variety of values and patterns in patches from different parts of the fabric so they give plenty of piecing mileage. Small prints help to camouflage patchwork seam-lines, so they are a good choice where you want to link the pieces on either side of a seam, where a large-scale print or a misaligned stripe would only emphasize the join.

"Scrap Quilt" by Kathy Home
Favorite fabrics left over from earlier quilts and some large-scale prints are combined for this scrap quilt. The main blocks are simple squares on point, given added interest with individual borders and yellow squares in the corners of alternate blocks giving a rhythm to the layout. Size 84 x 72 in (213 x 183 cm).

A detail from the "Scrap Quilt."

79
The scrap quilt effect

"Scrap quilts" use a lot of different fabrics together to create a more jumbled effect than other quilt designs (left). They often use a limited number of blocks, favoring repetition of only one or two units to give the design a sense of unity. Regain a sense of order by sorting your scraps and slightly limiting your color and fabric ranges. When you are making many identical blocks with assortments of different fabrics, don't worry about every block being a perfect combination. The blocks will be seen as a set rather than individually—unlike a single-block cushion, say—and the less successful ones will add to the quilt's charm. Study vintage quilts for inspiration—you will be surprised to see some quite ugly blocks in a quilt that is beautiful overall.

 TRY IT

80 Spice it up

Add some excitement and movement to your patchwork with stripes and checks, woven or printed (below). Cut stripes to give a sense of direction. You can keep woven stripes perfectly lined up by piecing with the striped fabric on top and sewing along the stripe. If you think this will be too difficult, cut pieces so the stripes are at right angles to the seam. Alternatively, don't worry about lining up stripes or checks and go for a casually off-grain look, but be careful not to stretch bias edges as you sew.

FIX IT

81 *Calm it down*

Checks and stripes used on the straight grain feel calm, but used on an angle they will feel busy and make your patchwork lively—which may not be the effect you want. If you are going to set patchwork blocks on point (see page 41), take this into consideration, as the check would end up on point too. Adding a simple striped border helps to define the quilt center and frame the blocks.

"Irori" (Hearth)
Repetition of the block and the use of only two units—a rectangle and a square—throughout this quilt help to keep the variety of stripes, checks, and print scales under control. One floral print fabric provided dark, medium, and light pieces when cut, so the three blocks look quite different. In deciding the layout, blocks made with the lightest fabrics were positioned first. Size 69 in (175 cm) square.

WORKING WITH QUILT PATTERNS

Whether you want to follow a complete pattern or design your own, you will need to make a plan or pattern for most quilt projects, from the traditional to modern.

Using a pattern

Quilt patterns have been published in books and magazines for well over 100 years. They can be a helpful resource, whether you choose to make the quilt as shown or change some features to make it more individual. Some professional quilters produce their own patterns, so there's lots of choice.

82 What's included

Unlike some nineteenth-century patterns which were often quite vague, modern books and magazines usually include cutting lists, instructions for any special techniques used, patchwork assembly instructions, diagrams, quilting suggestions, and more, along with color photographs of the completed project. Books are more likely to include step-by-step photographs and diagrams showing particular techniques, but some magazine projects include these too, particularly if the methods used are new or unusual. Information about the fabrics used and where to buy them (sometimes as a kit) may be added at the end of the pattern.

83 Golden rules

• Read through the whole pattern before you start and try to visualize the different stages involved.
• Pay attention to the skill level, if one is indicated. If it is graded "advanced" and you have only just begun quilting, you might want to add the pattern to your "future projects" folder or, at the very least, try out any new techniques on a small sample or single block first.
• Check through the requirements list for fabrics and equipment, so you don't get caught (frustratingly!) without that essential gadget half way through.
• Check the cutting list for the pattern. Cut out your fabrics and organize the cut pieces ready for sewing. If the quilt involves a complex block design that has a long cutting list, make a test

block to check you have understood the pattern correctly—you may be committing yourself to cutting out patches for dozens of blocks.
• Designers and editors welcome feedback. Let them know if you enjoyed using a pattern. They love to see photos of your completed quilts, especially if they are in a different colorway from the original or you have adapted the pattern in a unique way. Magazines may feature your version on their letters page.
• If you spot an error in the pattern—and occasionally, despite very careful proofreading, this does happen—it is worth contacting the designer or editor, who will be able to pass the information on in a future magazine issue or include an erratum slip in the pattern.

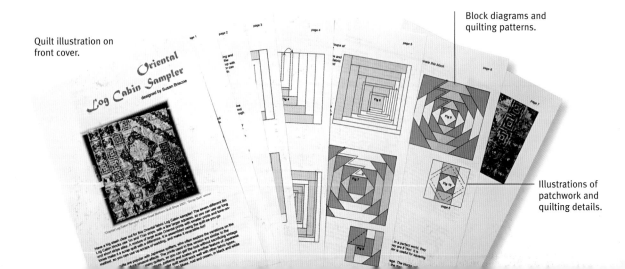

Block diagrams and quilting patterns.

Quilt illustration on front cover.

Illustrations of patchwork and quilting details.

▧ TRY IT

84 Adapting a pattern

Perhaps you would like a block-based quilt to be one patch larger or smaller—simply increase the number of blocks or patches used. Photocopy diagrams and any parts of the instructions you might want to annotate or alter, so you don't need to write notes on the original pattern.

Begin by roughly sketching your ideas on squared or isometric graph paper and make a cutting list for reference, amending the number of pieces you need to cut. You will need to alter border and backing sizes if you are changing the quilt's size. Altering the size of the block is another option, but you will need to resize all the cutting pieces too. Drawing out the block and noting down the new patch sizes is essential to avoid confusion over measurements. Trying to work out different patch sizes with the seam allowances included will result in mistakes, so work out the individual patch sizes without the seam allowances, enlarge or reduce the patches to the new block size, and then add the seam allowances to the measurements.

FIX IT

85 Substituting fabrics

If you like a design but don't like the materials used, make the quilt using fabrics you prefer. Substituting one patchwork fabric for another is quite straightforward, although you will need to plan carefully if you want to include a directional fabric like a stripe. Make notes about your fabric substitutions so you won't get mixed up when cutting out or sewing the patchwork. Changing tones in the design, especially switching dark and light fabrics, will make the patchwork look quite different and cause momentary confusion about which patch is which when you are assembling the patchwork. A block or patchwork sketch with the tones indicated will help.

"Black and White Quilt" (above left) and "Oriental Log Cabin Sampler" (below) by Betty Coops
The same Log Cabin variation blocks were used for both these quilts—the original in multicolored oriental scraps and Betty's version in black and white prints with touches of purple. Both use the same blocks in different arrangements. "Oriental Log Cabin" size 64 in (163 cm) square; "Black and White" size 80 x 64 in (203 x 163 cm).

Designing with traditional blocks

Block-format patchwork underwent a massive development in nineteenth-century North America—hundreds of blocks were designed, often with interesting names. They continue to inspire and influence quilters today, whether used in their traditional forms or adapted for contemporary styles.

Basic block grids

86 What's in a name?

Some blocks have more than one name (right), while others share the same one, such as the various blocks all called Split Nine Patch. While it is fun to find out about the history of a block name—and you may select a block for a particular project because the name is appropriate, such as Double Wedding Ring for an anniversary quilt—you don't have to become a block-name expert to enjoy making block patchwork designs.

87 Block types

Traditional patchwork blocks fall into several groups and are generally square:

Four-patch

Five-patch

Seven-patch

Nine-patch

One-patch blocks are made by repeating the same unit, such as One-patch Star.

Four-patch blocks, such as Broken Pinwheel, are made of four main square units. The squares can be subdivided.

Nine-patch blocks are made of nine units—usually square, or squares and rectangles combined. Squares can be subdivided.

Five-patch blocks, including Sister's Choice, are made on a 5 x 5 unit grid.

Seven-patch blocks, such as Bear's Paw, are made on a 7 x 7 unit grid. The squares can be subdivided.

Star blocks may be drafted on an eight-pointed star grid (see "Try it"), but also include nine-patch star blocks like Friendship Star.

Log Cabin blocks are sewn from a starting square, usually but not always in the center.

Fan blocks, such as Grandmother's Fan, have radiating designs, often from one corner.

Hexagonal and octagonal blocks frame the shape within a square. Draft octagonal blocks on an eight-pointed star grid.

Irregular blocks such as Snail Trail, don't fit any of the above groups.

88 One-patch patchwork

One-patch patchwork is made of a single patch unit repeated to make the whole design. The most basic example would be squares sewn together to make long strips, which are then sewn together to make a checkerboard patchwork. Hexagons and triangles can also be used for one-patch patchwork. What distinguishes a one-patch patchwork from a one-patch block is that the patches aren't assembled into blocks first.

FIX IT

91 Making templates

Simple paper folding is a good way to make templates for block types that don't fit readily into your chosen block size, such as a nine-patch block at 8 in (200 mm). Start with a piece of paper that is the same size as your finished block. For a nine-patch, fold the paper into thirds vertically (below); for a five-patch, fold into five; and so on. Open the paper out and fold the same divisions going across the paper. The crease-lines form the grid for drafting your block. Cut out pieces to use as paper templates, and cut out fabrics adding $\frac{1}{4}$ in (6 mm) all around the template (see page 48).

89 Playing with sizes

Four-, nine-, five-, and seven-patch blocks are easiest to make if you use a grid divisible by the relevant number. A nine-patch block works easily on a 6, 9, or 12 in (150, 230, or 300 mm) square; a five-patch on a 10 or 15 in (250 or 380 mm) square; and so on. If you want to combine blocks of different types in the same project—perhaps a sampler quilt where every block should be different—you will need to choose a block size that will work for each block. This may mean working with lots of quarter-inches, eighths, or even sixteenths to achieve the combination you want. Nine-patches and five-patches will work together on 7½ and 15 in (190 and 380 mm) blocks; nines and fours on 3, 6, 9, and 12 in (80, 150, 230, and 300 mm). More complex blocks are better in larger sizes—unless you want to make a miniature quilt, a finished 1-in (25-mm) half-square triangle or triangle square is about as small as you will want to piece. Consider repeating simple blocks, such as a basic nine-patch or four-patch, to match the size of single, more complicated blocks. Blocks that don't share compatible grids will give a fragmented effect where they meet—use sashing (see page 40) to reduce this effect if you don't like it.

92 Drafting blocks and the cutting list

Use graph paper to draft your block designs, so you can work out the sizes and numbers of the pieces you need to cut. Look at how many blocks are made up from easy-to-piece patchwork units, such as half-square triangles (or triangle squares) and Flying Geese. If you intend to use easy piecing methods to make these, as shown on pages 64 and 65, you can draw your block at a reduced scale as you won't need to use your drawing to make templates, only to note down the sizes of the pieces you need to cut. For more complex blocks where you need to use your drawing to make templates, draft the block full-size. List how many pieces you need of each size to make each block, and multiply these by the number of blocks you want to make. This is your cutting list.

TRY IT

90 Stars and octagons

Templates for eight-pointed stars and octagonal blocks can also be worked out by paper folding.

1 | First fold the paper into quarters (squares) and then fold it again diagonally, as shown.

2 | Make another diagonal fold, as shown.

3 | Open the paper out. You now have the foundation for drawing octagonal blocks, as shown by the extra lines on the paper.

4 | Make some extra folds for an eight-pointed star, folding across the paper from one octagon corner to the other, four times. Open the paper out and draw the eight-pointed star along the fold lines.

Planning a block quilt design

Blocks are arranged or "set" in various traditional ways to achieve different effects. Even the most unassuming block can make an interesting quilt with the right setting. Use sashing and other features to make the most of your patchwork.

 TRY IT

93 Using sashing

Sampler quilts, where all the blocks are different (below), usually use sashing to control and calm the block collection, visually linking a variety of patterns. Adding sashing to just two sides of each block—but alternating between top and bottom, and left and right—can liven up a sampler.

94 Straight settings

A straight setting is the simplest way to arrange your blocks. You will notice that the blocks form an all-over pattern or tessellation, achieving interesting optical effects. If you alternate between two blocks, an almost infinite number of patterns are possible.

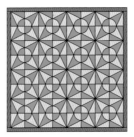

96 Checkerboard effect

Try alternating plain and pieced blocks in a checkerboard effect. This is a good way to reduce the amount of piecing you need to do for your quilt. Uneven numbers of blocks will produce the most appealing checkerboards, as all the corner blocks will be the same. The plain blocks can be printed fabric rather than a plain color, or try alternating appliqué and pieced blocks.

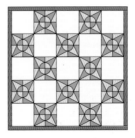

95 Sashing techniques

Sashing is a narrow strip between blocks. It is helpful for linking otherwise unrelated blocks (as in a sampler quilt), introducing another fabric, or simply providing some breathing space between blocks. Blocks are sewn together in strips with short sashing pieces in between, then the strips are sewn together with long sashing strips in between. The long strips are usually positioned horizontally, so they don't have to be the full length of the quilt. For more about sashing, see page 81.

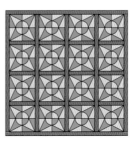

97 Adding posts

Posts are often added to sashing. These are small squares positioned at the points where the sashing strips meet. Posts mean long lengths of fabric are unnecessary for sashing and are a good way to introduce a contrasting accent fabric. Sashing with posts can be sewn to two sides of each block (three at the edge and four at the corner as required).

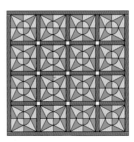

98 "On point" designs

Setting blocks "on point" often makes a design look livelier. The blocks are still sewn together in rows, but diagonally, with a half-block at each end. Unless your block is divided diagonally all the way through and you can simply assemble two halves or four quarters of the block for the edges and corners, you will need to add seam allowances to those pieces that touch the outer edge—simply cutting a completed block in half will mean there is no seam allowance at the edge of the patchwork and the points at the block corners will be lost in the border seam or in the binding if there is no border. All the settings already described can be used diagonally.

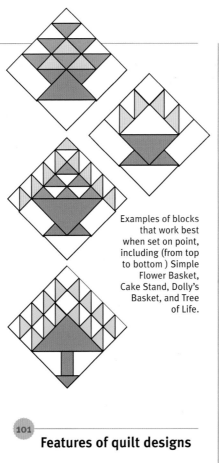

Examples of blocks that work best when set on point, including (from top to bottom) Simple Flower Basket, Cake Stand, Dolly's Basket, and Tree of Life.

100 Your quilt sketch

Sketch a plan of your quilt to help you visualize how the blocks will work together. Squared or graph paper makes this easy. Use a photocopier to make multiples of your block design, cutting out and pasting them to make an all-over plan. There are specialist quilt-design computer programs that will allow you to color in blocks with scans of the fabrics you plan to use. Color in an outline plan with pencils or fibertip pens to try out different color schemes. This will only give an approximation of your finished quilt's appearance, but it can be a useful planning tool. Simply indicating light, dark, and medium tones will suffice for scrap quilts, which combine dozens of fabrics arranged by tone.

101 Features of quilt designs

Traditional quilt designs make subtle use of some sophisticated design concepts. These include:
- Repetition—through the block design, the shapes used in the blocks, or the fabrics and symmetry in block arrangement.
- Symmetry—reflective (mirror images), rotational (blocks are rotated around a common center), or translated (blocks are repeated).
- Closure—patchwork quilts link individual elements (patches or blocks) so they appear as a single, recognizable pattern.
- Uniform connectedness—blocks or patches that are connected by the same visual properties, such as shape or color, appear more related than elements that are unique and are seen as a single, unified group.

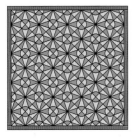

Computer design programs enable you to fill the blocks with fabric images.

■ TRY IT

99 Scaling

Don't automatically assume that what works for one block will work equally well at another size. A simple block like a basic nine-patch, in a small-scale print or plain fabric, will look more interesting at 6 in (150 mm) square than at 15 in (380 mm) square. A complex block with many pieces will work better at a larger size, unless you are aiming for a miniature quilt. A large-scale print may not look as good fragmented or cut into small pieces, so use it for larger pieces in a block or save it for the "plain" blocks in a setting.

"Koi Steps"
Large-scale oriental prints are shown off to best advantage with 8 in (200 mm) squares used as the "plain" squares in this checkerboard setting; smaller-scale coordinating patterns were used for the Courthouse Steps blocks. Quilt center, size 64 in (163 cm) square.

Style genres

There are differences and similarities between all the modern quilting genres—traditional, contemporary, art, innovative—and the boundaries are often blurred. This selection of quilts explores aspects of quilting design today.

"Perspective and Optical Illusion" by Pat Storey
Geometric quilts are not necessarily traditional. This contemporary example explores geometry by distorting the traditional block patchwork style. Machine-pieced and quilted. Size 24 in (61 cm) square.

"Liberty Jewel Box" by Dot Sherlock
The Jewel Box block glows with color from the Liberty cotton lawn used for this modern version of a traditional patchwork design. "Traditional" usually describes modern quilts made with a traditional block or motif. Machine pieced and quilted. Size 66 x 48 in (168 x 122 cm).

"Some Sisters Have No Choices" by Linda Bilsborrow
The quilter has conveyed a stark message with photo-printed fabric used for an otherwise traditional Sister's Choice block. Compare this with another quilt made for the same block challenge (page 32)—the second quilt alters the block more than this, but the photo prints give a contemporary interpretation. Machine pieced and quilted. Size 24 in (61 cm) square.

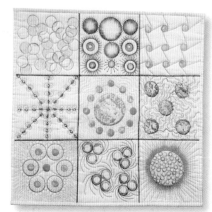

"Nine Patch" by Sheena Norquay
Stamped and painted calico has been machine quilted with metallic threads using the format of a nine-patch block but without patchwork. A contemporary quilt that reinterprets an old design, it is related to a larger piece entitled "Transforming Traditions." Machine pieced and quilted. Size 24 in (61 cm) square.

"Pink Paradise Birdsong"
1950s textile designs inspired this small art quilt wallhanging, machine appliquéd and hand quilted. The design has no traditional patchwork or quilting motifs, although the background hand quilting is inspired by Japanese sashiko (page 118). Size 32 x 21 in (81 x 53 cm).

"Velvet Parquet"
by Barbara Howell
A contemporary wallhanging based on traditional Rail Fence blocks. Hand-dyed velvets and machine-embroidered panels were combined with decorative machine quilting for a highly tactile surface. Size 60 x 40 in (152 x 102 cm).

"By the Green of the Spring"
Traditional blocks have been arranged in a contemporary layout for this small quilt made for a "New Beginnings" challenge. Machine pieced and quilted. Size 40 in (107 cm) square.

"Golden Fifties"
Katharine Guerrier's Color Block design was adapted for a modern retro design reminiscent of the 1950s. Machine-pieced and quilted as two large rectangles, each panel was cut into three triangles before rearrangement and assembly using the Quilt-as-you-go method (page 116). Size 72 in (183 cm) square.

Quilting inspirations

Many people want to try patchwork and quilting after seeing a traditional, antique, or vintage quilt. On these pages there is an introduction to just a few of the numerous patchwork and quilting traditions from around the world which are continued today.

 TRY IT

102 Researching vintage

If you love a particular style of vintage quilt and want to work in that style, it pays to research it via books, museum visits, and specialist quilting exhibitions. Discovering the history of a patchwork or quilting tradition is a fascinating pursuit in itself. You will be constantly surprised by the designs, needlework skills, and sheer inventiveness of previous quilting generations —especially when you consider that they did not have the resources of modern quilters.

103 Global traditions

There are many traditions worldwide to inspire you with their color and pattern combinations. Some traditions are associated with particular colors and fabrics, such as the plain fabrics used by Amish quilters and the red and green color schemes of Pennsylvania Dutch quilts. Baltimore album quilts, Hawaiian quilting, and the American patchwork block tradition are popular inspirations. Modern quilt fabrics reproduce vintage patterns, so achieving the right "look" is possible. Some European countries also have a rich quilting tradition that is worth exploring, and there are traditions from Asia as well.

Amish quilters, noted for their meticulous stitching, produce bold designs without using printed fabrics (top right).

A Hawaiian woman stitches a green quilt with traditional plant motifs.

Antique signature quilt.

104

Hexagons and coverlets

English paper piecing (see page 78) was favored for decorative patchwork from the early eighteenth century. Coverlets from this period show a taste for curves and complex designs, while during the nineteenth century patterns such as Grandmothers' Flower Garden—made from hexagons—and Tumbling Blocks—made from diamonds—were among the favorites. They were made from cotton prints or, later, silk and velvet. Fabrics reflected the dressmaking fashions of the day. Similar rich fabrics were used for late Victorian "Crazy Quilts," a style begun in the US.

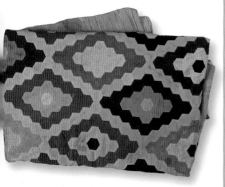

"Hexagon Diamonds,"
Poole family collection
This patchwork coverlet was made entirely of 1-in (25-mm) English paper-pieced hexagons, using fabric scraps from the family's rag bag.

FIX IT

105 *Recreating history*

The right fabrics and the right pattern are essentials for recreating a look. There are many ranges of reproduction fabrics of different eras, and searching out just the right fabrics will help you make your historically inspired quilt. Be aware that certain patchwork patterns are associated with different eras too—Dresden Plate was very popular in the 1930s, for example, while crazy patchwork in silks and velvets was popular in the late nineteenth century. Many block patterns were first published in American ladies' magazines dating from the late nineteenth and early twentieth centuries, and modern quilt block books will often record the earliest sources.

PATCHWORK.—SIZE AND DETAIL OF ONE SQUARE.

Early Log Cabin
The Ladies' Treasury, a popular English magazine of the 1870s, included instructions for "Mosaic Patchwork" in 1876. It is a version of the pattern we would recognize as Log Cabin.

Baltimore Album Quilt with floral and foliate decoration (left).

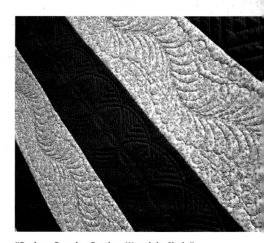

"Durham Running Feather, Weardale Chain"
by Lilian Hedley
Two traditional patterns from the Northeast of England on strippy patchwork, hand quilted.

CUTTING SKILLS

Accurate patchwork usually begins with accurate cutting, so you can piece your patchwork with a ¼-in (6-mm) seam allowance. Practice cutting to become more efficient and it will cease to be a chore.

Rotary cutting

Rotary cutting has revolutionized modern patchwork. It is more accurate and quicker than using scissors and templates. You can cut through more than one fabric layer at a time. It is even possible to combine rotary cutting with templates to cut shapes like hexagons.

106 Prepare your fabrics

• Make cutting easier by pressing your fabric smooth before you start, to remove any creases.
• It is easier to cut crisp fabric, so starch your fabrics before you begin. If you have prewashed them, you will have starched them already (see page 20).
• Layer your fabrics if you want to cut through several layers at once, aligning the selvedge. Practice first! Your rotary cutter blade needs to be sharp for this.
• Pressing the already pressed and layered fabric with a little steam will help the fabrics stay together while you cut.

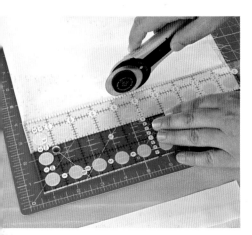

107 Cutting strips

With the ruler firmly on top of your fabric, square off uneven ends of the fabric, and cut off the tightly woven selvedge. Cut with the grain of the fabric (with printed stripes and checks, cut with the pattern). Turn your cutting mat through 180 degrees and line up the relevant mark along the ruler—for example, 2½ in (64 mm) if 2 in (50 mm) is the finished strip size. Line up your rotary cutter against the ruler's edge and cut, keeping the blade at right angles to the ruler edge—don't let it lean.

FIX IT

108 Wobbly edges?

Before you cut, check that the fabric is straight—it shouldn't be pulled or twisted to one side. Line up the ruler exactly where you want it on the fabric. Make sure the cutter blade stays in close contact with the side of the ruler while you cut and is at a 90-degree angle to the ruler edge. Whenever possible, cut with the fabric piece you need under the ruler—if you stray from the ruler's edge, you will only have cut into the waste fabric, and you can simply straighten up the cut.

109 Squares and rectangles

Cut strips economically to standard sizes for squares and rectangles, such as 2½-in (64-mm) squares and 1½ x 2½-in (38 x 64-mm) rectangles from the same 2½-in (64-mm) strip, as shown.

110 Triangles from squares and rectangles

1 | Cut along one diagonal to make a half-square triangle, lining up the 45-degree angle on your ruler with the edge of the square.

2 | Cut again for quarter-square triangles. Check instructions when cutting triangles from rectangles; sometimes the diagonal line will slope to the right, sometimes to the left.

111 Miters, triangles, and diamonds

1 | Miter the ends of rectangles by lining up the 45-degree line on the ruler with the bottom edge of the fabric.

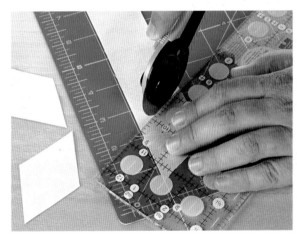

2 | The 60-degree line on the ruler can be used the same way to cut equilateral triangles and diamonds from a strip.

112 What to do with cut pieces

Organize cut pieces in shallow cardboard boxes, plastic trays, or similar; or store block components in ziplock plastic bags—there's nothing more annoying than a mislaid patch when you are sewing the pieces together!

▓ TRY IT

113 Conserving your mat

Cut with the ruler's measurements, not the mat's. If you repeatedly cut along the same measurement lines on your mat, eventually the cuts won't heal up and you will have a permanent gouge in the mat, making your cutter apparently skip threads when you cut across the gouge. Using the measurements on your ruler whenever possible, rather than those on the mat, or turning the mat over and using the other side will help it last longer.

Making templates

Before the rotary cutter was invented, patchwork required templates to cut the various pieces, and you will find them useful for many patchwork designs to this day. If you can make your own templates, you can make a patchwork pattern any size you like.

114

Drafting the pattern

You may find it easier to draft the pattern out full size before you begin; but as most blocks are made from several repeated shapes it is not necessary to cut templates for every piece of the block. Make one template for each shape. If there are mirror-images of some pieces, make a note on your cutting list that you need to flip the template over to cut some pieces. Alternatively, cut these with the fabric folded double (right) so you will have a mirror-image of each patchwork piece. Store template sets in clear plastic pockets, labeled with the block name and size for future reference, and label individual pieces too in case they get mixed up.

116

Working with paper templates

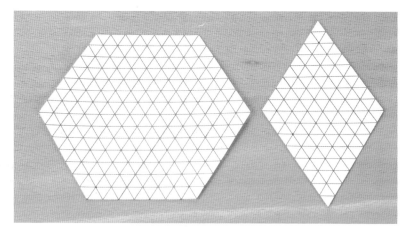

FIX IT

115 *Using plastic*

Thin template plastic is more robust and long-lasting than cardboard, but just as easy to cut out with a pair of scissors or a craft knife. It is available with a preprinted square or isometric grid, so you can simply cut along the lines.

You can use thin paper templates under a quilter's rule to remind you where to cut. Any template used this way needs to be thin enough to go under the ruler without making a bump. Cut pieces from graph paper to the sizes you need (above), remembering to add on the $\frac{1}{4}$-in (6-mm) seam allowance all around. You can combine pieces cut with templates and others cut with the rotary cutter and ruler in the same block—there is no need to make templates for squares and rectangles for machine piecing, where you will be using the edge of the patches as a guide for your $\frac{1}{4}$-in (6-mm) foot.

117
Hexagons, triangles, and diamonds

Cut out a paper hexagon template to the required size—
isometric graph paper is useful for this. Stick the template to
the underside of the ruler temporarily (below), lining up with
the edge and the 60-degree line. Cut hexagons from a fabric
strip, lining up the template and ruler for each cut. This method
is also good for triangles and diamonds.

118
Sturdy cardboard templates

You can make more substantial templates from thin card, cutting
it with a pair of scissors or a metal ruler and a craft knife. With
the template on the fabric, draw around it with a fine pencil
(below) and cut out along the line with a pair of scissors. Be
careful not to press in the template edges with the pencil point,
or it will become increasingly smaller and inaccurate as you mark!

▣ TRY IT

119 Reusing packaging

Collect recycled materials for making templates. Many
of the thin plastics and cards used for packaging are
ideal. They can also be used to make quilt-marking
templates. Save translucent plastic lids from coffee cups
and snack packaging too, as these make excellent circle
templates for appliqué.

120
Readymade options

Metal templates for popular patch sizes are a traditional way to
mark and cut patchwork. They are very useful for English paper
piecing, as the inner section is used to cut very accurate pieces
(see page 79) while the outer section can be used to frame
up a piece of fabric for fussy cutting (see page 50). Acrylic
templates allow you to see the fabric through the template
as you cut. Some are designed for rotary cutting, including
complete sets to make several different traditional blocks. If you
are going to make a lot of one particular block design and size,
sets like this would be a good investment, but for a one-off,
making your own is more economical.

Fussy cutting and kaleidoscope effects

Selecting particular parts of a print when cutting out gives scope for some very interesting effects, including kaleidoscopic designs. The Stack-n-Whack® method also produces a kaleidoscope effect, but achieved in an easier way. Whichever you try, be prepared for stunning results!

121
Fussy cutting

Use the "window" section from a template set to select an interesting part of the fabric pattern (right). Mark around the template and cut out. You can also select part of the pattern by simply viewing through your clear acrylic quilter's ruler. Large motifs may be displayed more effectively like this—particularly figures and animals, which you probably don't want to cut up. Remember that a quarter-inch of pattern will be lost in the seam allowance all around the piece.

"Japanese Sunrise" by Jennifer Lewis
Equilateral triangles are arranged for an abstract view of Mount Fuji, using Maxine Rosenthal's "One Block Wonders" technique. Size 38 x 29 in (97 x 74 cm).

122
Using kaleidoscope effects

Cutting the same area of fabric and arranging the pieces around the block can give various effects. This method is often seen on antique hexagon coverlets, where the pieces may be cut and arranged to give the impression of an opening flower, or with stripes in the fabric arranged in the same direction throughout the block. Turning the outer pieces on their side will produce a spinning effect and a feeling of movement.

Details from the "Japanese Sunrise" quilt.

123 Stack-n-Whack®

Stack-n-Whack® is an easy way to create stunning blocks with kaleidoscope effects, devised by Bethany Reynolds. Rather than fussy-cutting each piece, a number of identical, large-print fabrics are layered and cut together. When identical pieces from each layer are arranged in various patterns, the kaleidoscope effect is revealed. Some of Bethany's popular designs include fans and the double pinwheel, shown below. Don't prewash your fabric for this technique, as it may distort the pattern slightly and make it difficult to achieve the effect. For more information about this technique, see Useful addresses, page 156.

1 | Select a bold, strong print with plenty of contrast—this will show up the Stack-n-Whack® effect best. For the pinwheel design shown here, cut an 8¾-in (222-mm) square of fabric and use this to cut seven more squares, matching the print exactly each time. Layer the squares, checking they are all the same way up. Cut through the whole stack on both diagonals, and cut through the center horizontally and vertically. Each stack of triangles includes all the fabric pieces for your block.

2 | Arrange the triangles. All the triangles will need the background fabric added. Cut a 4¼-in (108-mm) square and quarter it diagonally to make the background triangles. Choose a background that complements but doesn't compete with your Stack-n-Whack® fabrics. Sew the pieces together in pairs to make four squares, then sew the squares together, as if to make a four-patch block. Set the blocks for your quilt top.

▪ TRY IT

124 Printing kaleidoscopes

Print your own fabrics for a special kaleidoscope effect (see pages 24–25). Using a photo album program on the computer, arrange multiples of small images on one sheet—enough to make the block. For 1-in (25-mm) hexagons, it is economical to print two sets of six pieces on each letter-size (A4) sheet, with a separate sheet for the individual center pictures.

FIX IT

125 Be bold!

Large-scale prints work best for kaleidoscope arrangements, as smaller designs and mini-prints are too homogenous in pattern—one part looks just like the next. Batiks and hand dyes are also unsuitable, because the patterns aren't true repeats.

PATCHWORK TECHNIQUES

Many of the same techniques are shared by both traditional and contemporary styles. You will find the solution to your patchwork needs among them.

Machine patchwork

The earliest machine-sewn quilts are almost as old as the domestic sewing machine, so machine patchwork has a long history. It is the most popular method for sewing patchwork today.

⬜ TRY IT

126 Straight stitching

Replacing the standard zigzag machine throat plate with a straight-stitch plate will improve your stitching. The needle cannot be accidentally dragged sideways, giving a better straight stitch and reducing the tendency for stitches to get "chewed up" at the start of a seam.

Straight-stitch throat plate

127 Laying out the block

Lay out the pieces before you begin sewing (above), and join them together following the individual block instructions. Many blocks require pieces to be sewn together in rows first.

128 Setting up the machine

Machine-sewn patchwork is relatively quick to do. Shorten the length of the machine stitch to around two-thirds of the normal length, to around 12–14 stitches per inch. Use a ¼-in (6-mm) seam allowance throughout. For most piecing, the stitches will start and finish at the edge, where the thread ends will be trapped by subsequent piecing, so there is no need to start and finish with backstitches (inset seams, see page 72, are the exception).

Machine piecing

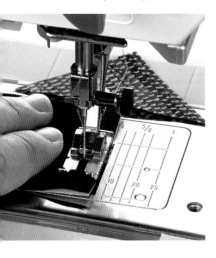

Place your first two pieces right sides together, making sure the edges to be sewn line up. Use the ¼-in (6-mm) foot and line up the fabric edge with the edge of the foot when you sew (left). It may help if you sit slightly to the right of the machine needle so you can see this easily. Use a fabric scrap as a "leader," so the first patchwork stitches don't get chewed up. Longer pieces will need to be pinned—always pin at right angles to the stitching line and remove pins as you sew. Hitting a pin as you sew will break the tip off the machine needle.

FIX IT

130 *Pressing toward darks*

Even with the best quality fabrics, dark colors may show through paler colors, so press toward the darker fabric whenever possible. Check the translucency of your patchwork against the batting and backing—laying the block directly on a dark-colored table or your green cutting mat may make the shadowing look worse than it really is.

Pressing techniques

Press each stage of your patchwork as you go, with the seam allowance to one side. Pressing in alternate directions encourages the seams to interlock neatly, as shown below. For blocks pieced from the center outward, such as Log Cabin (see page 59), press seams toward the outside of the block.

Pressing the seams to one side goes back to the American method of hand piecing; pressing them open would allow the batting to form "bearding" or work its way through the running stitched seam. As the machine stitched seam will be tighter and firmer than hand sewing, this is less of a risk, and modern batting is less likely to beard than the loose-fiber batting used 100 years ago. Occasionally you may have to press a seam open to reduce bulk.

Press with a dry iron or with a little steam, using an up-and-down action so the patchwork is not stretched and distorted—remember you are pressing, not ironing!

Press toward the darker fabric for preference, as pressing dark toward light can cause a shadow effect on paler fabrics.

"Kasuri Sampler Quilt"
A sampler of machine-pieced blocks inspired by antique Japanese fabrics and sashiko stitched blocks has strong tonal contrasts between the dark blue and cream fabrics. Pressing the seams toward the darker fabrics each time prevented shadowing behind the cream. Size 77 x 59 in (196 x 150 cm).

American patchwork

American hand-pieced patchwork (or simply American patchwork) is the hand-sewn ancestor of machine piecing, usually with a ¼-in (6-mm) seam. It requires neat, small running stitches but many quilters consider it to be an easier way to sew part-sewn seams (page 70), curves (page 74–77), and miters (page 73). Of course, it is portable too.

Seam allowance

Stitching line

Cutting the pieces

Pieces may be cut using templates or with a rotary cutter. If templates are used, some quilters prefer to leave the seam allowance off the template. Placing the template on the back of the fabric, draw around it with a sharp pencil. Remove the template and cut the piece out by hand, adding a ¼-in (6-mm) seam allowance by eye—if this is difficult, use a ruler or a ¼-in (6-mm) bar to add the seam allowance first.

If you cut your pieces with a ruler and a rotary cutter or use templates with the seam allowance added, you will need to draw the stitching line in pencil on the back of your fabric (above). Some readymade templates have holes in the corners so you can mark a dot at the start and finish of the stitching line first.

Pinning the pieces

Accurate pinning is very important for this technique. The method described here can also be used for greater accuracy in machined patchwork. After all, you need to line up those stitching lines accurately.

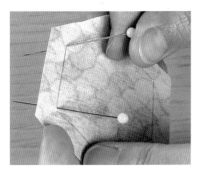

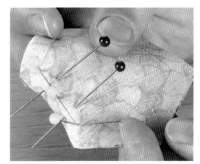

1 | Push a pin through each end of the line on the first patchwork piece, as shown.

2 | Hold the second patchwork piece under the first one, right sides together, and push the pins through the ends of the line on that piece too. The fabrics should be held close together.

3 | These first pins are holding the two pieces so the stitching lines are lined up correctly. Without removing the original pins, pin the two pieces together at right angles to the stitching line. Don't push the original pins through in the same way—that will actually push the stitching lines out of alignment, as one piece of fabric will almost invariably slip.

134 Stitching your patchwork

Start with a small knot and several backstitches. Use very small running stitches with an occasional backstitch along the stitching line only. You will be starting and finishing on the line, not going out to the edge of the seam allowance as you would for machine sewn patchwork. Finish as you started, with several backstitches and a small knot. Press seam allowances to one side, toward the darker fabric (see page 53).

Japanese Blues
Hand piecing American-style is very popular among Japanese quilters, enabling them to use vintage and antique fabrics that may be too fragile for machine stitching. Various kinds of indigo-dyed cottons are included in this anonymous small quilt. Size 28 x 22 in (71 x 56 cm).

Traditional indigo shibori tie-dye is used in this block.

TRY IT

135 Working on the move

American hand-pieced patchwork may appear a more time-consuming method of piecing than using the sewing machine but, like English paper piecing, it is very portable and you will be able to work in spare moments or even in front of the television. Try keeping a few blocks of your current project boxed up and ready to go in a sandwich tub with a small sewing kit, so you can take it wherever you go, and your patchwork will grow quickly.

FIX IT

136 Waxing thread

If you have problems with your thread knotting and looping as you sew, try taming it with beeswax or silicone wax before sewing (see page 11).

Easy blocks with squares and rectangles

Many blocks are constructed from only squares and rectangles; they are simple to make and are all you need to show off an attractive choice of fabric. Individual patch sizes are easy to work out if you are designing your own quilt and want to resize a block.

FIX IT

137 *Pinning*

It is fine to pin patchwork pieces, and you will be able to make longer strips match up with the edges of the block. Start by pinning the ends of the strip to the ends of the block (below), then add more pins along the strip, easing the two together if necessary. Always position pins at right angles to the seam. Although you can machine over pins, with the shorter stitch length you are using for machine patchwork there is an increased risk of hitting a pin and breaking the tip of the needle, so for complete safety, remove the pins as you go.

Many more complex blocks use the four-patch construction, although the individual squares are also made up of patchwork.

138 Four-patch blocks

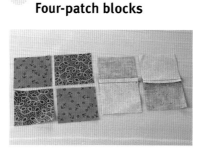

1 | Arrange pairs of squares as shown, place right sides together, and sew. Press seams in opposite directions. Place the two patchwork pieces right sides together—it will be possible to butt the previous seams together neatly, because the seam allowances lie on opposite sides of the seams.

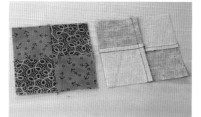

2 | Sew and press seam to one side. The seam allowances will line up perfectly!

139 Nine-patch blocks

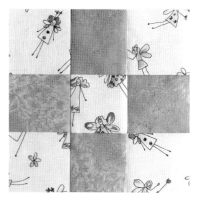

Arrange the pieces, sew into strips of three patches, and press seams to one side. Pressing all seams toward the darker fabric is best. Assemble the rest of the block following the instructions for Four-patch.

Like Four-patch, many blocks are made using the Nine-patch sequence, with the "patches" made of other patchwork units.

140 Log Cabin variations

Log Cabin blocks have strips sewn around the center block.

1 ▮ Pin the first strip to the center square and sew the strip. Press seams toward the outside of the block.

2 ▮ Pin and sew the second strip.

3 ▮ The Log Cabin light and dark effect is created by sewing the strips in pairs around the block. Continue adding strips in this way until the block is complete.

📖 TRY IT

141 Working out strip lengths

Some quilters prefer to sew consecutive strips to their Log Cabin block and trim them to length after sewing. Machine sewn strips tend to end up slightly overlong, as the machine feed dogs will pull through more fabric underneath than on top, and the finished block will have wavy edges. The more strips, the worse the waviness. It is easy to work out the length of strips needed for Log Cabin blocks and its variations, like Chevron Log Cabin, Courthouse Steps, and Off-center Log Cabin. Begin with a sketch on squared paper showing the block at the finished size, for example 10 in (254 mm) square, and draw the "log" strips, working inward. Use an easy strip width, like 1 in (25 mm), so the cut width will be 1½ in (38 mm). Working from your sketch and counting the number of squares in each strip, make a list of the number of light strips and dark strips you need, adding ½ in (13 mm) to the length of each strip for piecing.

Precut your fabric strips for perfect Log Cabin and variation blocks. Clockwise from top left: Log Cabin, Off-center Log Cabin, Corner in the Cabin (Chevron Log Cabin), and Courthouse Steps.

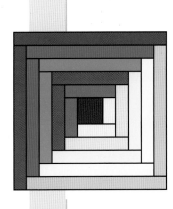
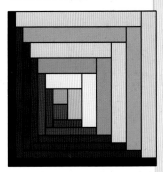
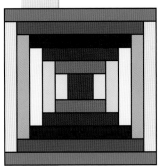
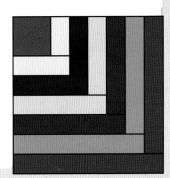

Improving your piecing speed

A little basic efficiency in sewing your machine patchwork can make a considerable difference to your productivity and help you keep your work organized. If you are fitting patchwork into a busy schedule, you'll be able to do more in the same amount of time—a real bonus when attending classes and workshops too.

FIX IT

142 *Working logically*

Machine sew your patchwork pieces in a logical order. Don't just mix everything up at random. If you have followed the instructions for laying out the pieces in the block (see page 52), you can begin by organizing the pieces for your blocks. For example, if your block designs involve sewing small four-patch units for the block corners, deal with all of them first. Make small heaps of patches for each block and work through these a block at a time, chain piecing. Don't snip the thread between sets of patches—keep going until you have finished sewing all of this stage and you have a long chain of units for your blocks. Cut the pieces off the chain, one block's-worth at a time, cutting and pressing the first block's units before moving on to the second, and so on. You are less likely to lose a unit between your sewing area and your ironing board and your units are organized for the next stage of your patchwork.

143

Chain piecing in a nutshell

Chain piecing is an industrial machining method that has been adopted for machine sewing patchwork. It saves time and thread, and can also help to keep your piecing organized. When you have sewn your first two pieces together, don't cut the thread. Place the next two pieces together and sew them a stitch or two after the first two pieces. Continue like this to make a "chain" which can be cut up afterward (right).

145

Two at a time

Continuing the chain-piecing theme, if you have a lot of blocks to sew you may find it easiest to work on two blocks at a time. In the early stages, there will be lots of pieces to sew together. As you get toward the end of your patchwork piecing, sew a piece to the first block and then sew its twin to the second block, chain piecing between the two. As you finish the second block, start on the next pair.

"Boromono" (Scrap Thing)
Going a step further with pieced strips and scraps, this wallhanging was made from recycled fabrics arranged in wide strips. Big-stitch quilting adds a country effect. Size 22 x 35 in (56 x 89 cm).

TRY IT

144 Saving thread

Save thread by chain piecing. Instead of having to snip off long threads at the start and end of each block, you only have to cut the pieces apart. You could save up to 50 percent of your piecing thread. That's a lot of thread!

146

Quick-pieced random Log Cabin

As an extension of the chain piecing method, try sewing a random Log Cabin design using scrap strips. The method isn't as accurate as sewing Log Cabin with pre-cut strips and you will probably quickly mix up the light and dark strips, but it produces a wonderful scrap quilt in a relaxed, innovative style. Use the walking foot rather than the ¼-in (6-mm) foot for this method, so the patchwork pieces and the strip are fed through the machine at the same rate.

1 ❙ Start with a long strip and several smaller squares or rectangles, or a mixture of both. Place the first patch on the strip, right sides together, and sew. As you finish sewing the first patch, place the next patch on the strip with only a fraction of an inch gap and sew the second patch to the strip. Continue until the patches are sewn down the full length of the strip. Cut the strip to separate the units, as shown. Press the seam toward the strip. Trim each piece so the ends of the strip match the ends of the initial square or rectangle.

2 ❙ Take a second strip and sew the patchwork units to this strip, rotating the pieces so you are, in effect, adding a second strip around the center square or rectangle patch. Once you have finished, cut the strip and press, as before.

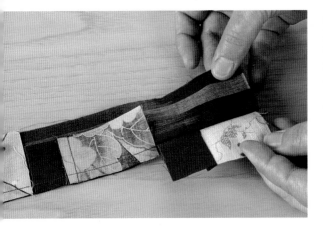

3 ❙ Continue adding strips to the block in this way, working around the block in a spiral. The block will increase in size so you will need to have more than one strip per step. It will also start to become irregular, so when your blocks have reached the size you want to make, trim them square.

4 ❙ The blocks can be trimmed to different sizes—say 6 in (150 mm), 6½ in (165 mm), and 7 in (178 mm) if this is going to be most economical—and sewn together in groups of the same size, building up the sizes of these completed groups with extra strips or trimming them down to join another set. If you want this irregular patchwork to have a more controlled look, use the fabric you have made to cut a series of squares all the same size, cutting them on a slant for more interest, and piece them back together with sashing strips.

Seminole and string patchwork

Both these speedy techniques involve sewing strips together, which are then cut and rearranged to make other patterns. They must be machine sewn because the seams are cut across and hand sewing would come undone.

FIX IT

147 *Avoiding ripples*

After several long strips are sewn together by machine, you will notice the patchwork tends to ripple—one side will be longer than the other or, if you have been sewing strips on either side of a central strip, these may be longer. This is caused by the machine's feed dogs feeding the lower layer of fabric through the machine at a slightly faster rate than the top one. Use a walking foot when sewing long strips to help reduce the problem, as both fabrics will be fed through at the same rate. Sewing strips together in pairs, then sewing one pair to another pair, and so on, also helps.

148 Seminole basics

This is a machine piecing technique that originated with the American Seminole Indians, who use bright, plain fabrics to make strips to decorate clothing as well as quilts. It can speed up piecing some patchwork blocks made from squares and rectangles. Long strips are machine sewn together before being cut into slices and rearranged to make new patterns.

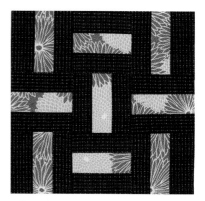

1 | Rotary cut strips to the required width and sew them together. Press the seams to one side. Rotary cut slices, cutting across the sewn seam (above). Remember to add the seam allowance before you cut—the pieces in the picture are 3½ in (90 mm) square. Rearrange the pieces to make your block and sew together.

2 | Rotate, flip, or offset the pieces to make other patchwork patterns. You may need to trim the edges straight after piecing for any offset designs. Take care not to stretch any bias edges left exposed this way and leave an adequate seam allowance so you don't "chop off" points in the seam allowance later.

The Seminole technique is particularly useful for variations on the traditional Rail Fence block, as shown at right.

String patchwork

149

Narrow strips or "strings" are sewn together in a similar manner to Seminole piecing, but to make a wider piece of patchwork which can be cut to make sections for other blocks. String patchwork is an interesting way to use up random strips and thin wedges of fabric, giving a lively effect, and it is an ideal scrap project.

▦ TRY IT

150 **Creating units**

With a little planning, the Seminole technique can be used to create units for many blocks, such as these blocks from traditional Japanese designs. Using Seminole patchwork to make sections with ½-in (13-mm) squares and strips is easier than trying to sew 1-in (25-mm) squares together accurately.

"Igeta" (Well Curb)
The basic Seminole method was used to make these block centers. No squares were cut individually—five strips were sewn together for each block, cut into three slices, and sewn together with long strips in between. Size 63 in (160 cm) square.

Easy triangles

Sewing these triangles into squares is easy—you don't have to worry about stretching one bias edge when sewing it to another, because the edge is cut after it is sewn. A similar method makes fast corners for octagonal designs.

FIX IT

151 *Checking sizes*

Do your half square triangles come out smaller than expected? You may be sewing a larger seam allowance than necessary. If you can't fix it by checking your seam allowance, add an extra ½ in (13 mm) rather than ⅜ in (10 mm) and trim your blocks to size after piecing.

153 Controlling bias edges

You will probably already know how much a bias edge can stretch—just think of bias tape. Fabrics with a lower thread count, such as the cotton flannels used for country-style quilts, are particularly prone to stretching along a bias edge. Once stretched, it is almost impossible to persuade the edge to go back to its original shape and the waviness won't disappear completely even with the most careful pressing. For this reason, any bias on the edge of a block must be handled carefully while it is exposed, as in the block below. Cutting the bias edge after sewing is one way to control this problem.

152 Half-square triangles

This accurate method of making half-square triangles (also called triangle squares) avoids the necessity of sewing two bias-cut edges together, as the cut is made after the diagonal lines are sewn. Use it to make half-square triangle units for blocks, including those made completely from half-square triangles, like Pinwheel and Broken Dishes. Start by adding an extra ⅜ in (10 mm) to the usual ¼ in (6 mm) all-round seam allowance to the desired finished size of your square—so, for a 4-in (102-mm) finished square, cut 4⅞-in (124-mm) squares, not 4½-in (114-mm) squares as you would normally.

1 Draw a diagonal line on the lighter square and place the squares together. Treat the line as the fabric edge, aligning it with the edge of the ¼-in (6-mm) foot, and machine sew with a ¼-in (6-mm) seam. Sew again along the other side of the drawn line and cut along the line.

2 Open out both half-square triangles and press toward the darker fabric. Clip off the "dog ears"—trim the ends of the seams flush with the edges of the square. This makes two half-square triangles or triangle squares.

154 Quarter-square triangles

These are easy to make by repeating the steps above using the half-square triangles you have already made. Remember to add the diagonal seam allowance twice to the size of your original pieces, so add ⁷⁄₁₀ in (19 mm) rather than ⅜ in (10 mm) this time.

1 Place one of the half-square triangles on top of the other, with the darker triangle on top of the lighter one, and vice versa. Mark the diagonal line again and sew down either side, as before.

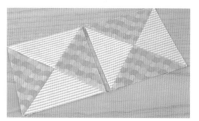

2 Cut and press. You will have two quarter square triangles, as shown.

155

Fast corners

Add triangles to corners of a square, like sewing the Flying Geese units to make a diamond in a square.

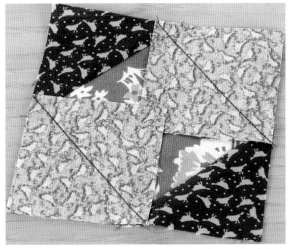

1 **I** Cut squares half the size of the finished block plus ½ in (12 mm) for seam allowances. For example, cut a 2½-in (64-mm) square if your finished square size will be 4 in (102 mm)—your square will be cut 4½ in (114 mm) to start with. Draw a diagonal line on each small square. Place one square on the corner as shown and sew along the drawn line.

2 **I** Fold over the triangle you have made and press. Use scissors to trim away the excess fabric underneath and repeat. If the block is large enough, sew a second line and make little half-square triangles (see Try It).

3 **I** Use this method to add triangles to just two corners of the square, for blocks like Prairie Flowers. Triangles are added along one edge for the beige patches and to opposite corners for the corner pieces. Using the corner pieces from this block as a block in its own right produces a striking tessellated slanted star design.

4 **I** Sew smaller squares to the corners to make octagonal blocks.

"Miniature Chevrons"
Made from triangles trimmed from other blocks, this miniature dollhouse quilt is ¹⁄₁₂ scale. Size 4½ in (11.4 cm) square.

TRY IT

156 **Making chevrons**

Striped fabrics make interesting patterns when used for half-square triangles, as they will produce a chevron effect (below). This can be emphasized as a design feature in your blocks by carefully matching the stripes on each patch when cutting out.

Flying Geese variations

This easy method of making a triangle on the corner of another patch is the key to making Flying Geese, parallelograms, octagons in squares, and squares on point. Once again, there's no sewing bias edges!

TRY IT

157 Saving triangles

If you are making larger Flying Geese, don't waste the triangles you cut off. Draw a second sewing line ½ in (13 mm) from the first, on the part you are going to cut off and sew before cutting the triangle off. You will have a small half-square triangle, which can be used for another block.

158

Introducing a classic block

The classic rectangular unit can be made in several ways. Using three triangles would mean sewing bias edges (see page 62). It is much simpler to make it using a combination of squares and rectangles, trimming the pieces as you go. The first method is good for using up smaller scraps, as the base is a rectangle, while the second—although it uses a larger square patch at the beginning—is more economical overall. Flying Geese can be used on their own, in rows for borders, or as component units for other blocks, such as Art Square and Album Star. They also make great "roofs" for little houses.

Many blocks use Flying Geese units for star and diamond effects.

159

Flying Geese: method one

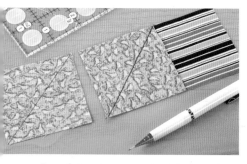

1 ❙ Cut out a rectangle, ½ in (13 mm) longer and wider than the finished size of your Flying Geese unit. Cut two squares the same size as the shorter rectangle measurement. For example, for a finished size of 4 x 2 in (102 x 50 mm) cut a rectangle 4½ x 2½ in (114 x 64 mm) plus two 2½ in (64 mm) squares. Draw a diagonal line on each square.

2 ❙ Right sides together, place one square on the rectangle and sew along the drawn line. Fold over the triangle you have made, and press. Use scissors to trim away the excess fabric underneath.

3 ❙ Repeat with the second triangle. This method is an easy way to make Flying Geese from smaller scraps, with minimal wastage—try the Saving triangles method (157, above) for no leftovers at all.

160

Flying Geese: method two

This makes four Flying Geese units with no waste—ideal for blocks that require sets of four.

1 | Cut out a square, 1¼ in (32 mm) larger than the longest side of your finished Flying Geese unit. Cut four squares, ⅞ in (22 mm) larger than the shortest side of the finished unit. For example, for a finished size of 4 x 2 in (102 x 50 mm) cut one 5¼-in (133-mm) square plus four 2⅞-in (73-mm) squares.

Draw a diagonal line on each square. With right sides together, place two smaller squares on the large square. Treating the drawn line as the fabric edge, line it up with the edge of the ¼-in (6-mm) foot, and machine sew with a ¼-in (6-mm) seam allowance. Sew again along the other side of the drawn line.

2 | In a variation from the previous method, cut along the drawn line, dividing the patchwork into two large triangles. Flip the resulting smaller triangles outward, and press. Cutting the first line at this stage removes the problem of trying to pin the first set of triangles out the way while sewing the second.

3 | Place the two remaining squares on the large triangles as shown and sew along either side of the drawn line as before. When finished, cut along the line, flip the smaller triangles outward and press. You should have four triangle squares.

161

Parallelograms

You can make other units for use in patchwork blocks by following the first method for Flying Geese. Pieced Star Variation (right) uses parallelograms, made by sewing the second triangle so the seam slopes in the same direction as the first, as shown below.

The same set of Flying Geese can be used to make various blocks, depending on how they are arranged.

Easy foundation piecing

You can make patchwork quickly and easily with foundation piecing. Pieces
are machine sewn together onto a paper or fabric foundation, which stabilizes
the fabric—so it's good for those hard-to-piece fabrics like silk.

TRY IT

162 Quilt-as-you-go

Simple foundation-pieced
patchwork is ideal for making
sections for quilt-as-you-go
projects, if the patchwork is
sewn onto batting as well as
backing so it is pieced and
quilted in one go. See page 116
for more about quilt-as-you-go.

163 Working a patchwork strip

This method is the most basic form of foundation piecing and an easy method for
scraps. Cut a foundation strip from plain calico or similar fabric slightly larger than
required. If you want to keep your strips lined up straight, try using a fabric with
a pale stripe instead of calico.

1 ▌ Cut an assortment of patchwork
pieces in various widths—the length
should be the same or slightly longer
than the foundation strip width. Place
the first piece face up on the end of the
foundation strip and line up the edges.

2 ▌ Place the second piece face down on
the first piece, pin and machine sew the
two pieces together with a ¼-in (6-mm)
seam along the long edge only, so you
have sewn through the foundation strip
as well.

3 ▌ Flip the second piece over so
the right side is showing, and press.
Continue adding pieces in the same
way until the whole foundation strip
is covered. Trim to the size required.

The strips don't have to be exactly
parallel. Try angling them slightly
for a pleasingly random look.

164 Foundation-pieced patchwork

Sewing patchwork onto a foundation keeps it under control, so this method is suitable for trickier fabrics such as silk, velvet, and fabrics that are less stable; as well as cotton strips. A fabric foundation is left in place, helping to support the patchwork, but you can also use a tear-off paper foundation, which would be removed before quilting. Special foundation papers and non-woven fabrics are available, which can be removed easily by tearing. Simple foundation piecing is also known as stitch and flip. Using a calico foundation will make your patchwork two fabric-layers thick, so use sashing rather than joining pieces directly with a bulky seam. This is also a good technique for patchwork bags, as a calico foundation supports the patchwork and makes the bag stronger.

FIX IT

165 *Piecing strips*

The foundation should be adequately covered with strips, so join shorter pieces together before you start. Pieced strips can add an interesting effect, making the patchwork look complex and exciting, as seen in the example at right.

166 Log Cabin on foundation

Log Cabin is often stitched on a foundation and has been made this way for well over 100 years—it is the "Mosaic Patchwork" shown in *The Ladies' Treasury* magazine in 1876, where the foundation is used to control the dress silks used for their project (see page 45).

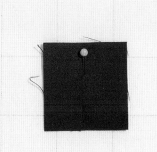

1 | Mark guidelines for Log Cabin on a fabric foundation backing—for example, consecutive squares at 1-in (25-mm) intervals for 1-in (25-mm) strips. Cut strips ½ in (13 mm) wider than the finished size. The center square can be the same size as the strip width, so the first strip will be the same size as the square, or larger. Pin the center square piece in place. Log Cabin centers in old quilts are usually a bright or light color.

2 | Pin, machine stitch, and flip the first strip. Use the guidelines on the foundation square to help align the strips. For non-foundation pieced Log Cabin (see page 57), the light and dark effect is created by sewing the strips in pairs around the block. Start with light strips if you want the darker tone to predominate, or dark strips if you want more light tone. Contrast shiny silks and matte cotton fabrics for a different effect.

3 | Pin, machine stitch, and flip the second strip. Continue adding strips in this way until the block is complete.

Further foundation piecing

Foundation piecing can be the solution to various super-sharp patchwork effects when the design is marked on a translucent tear-away stabilizer and the patchwork is sewn from the back. It can be combined with other machine piecing, widening your patchwork possibilities.

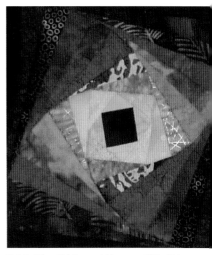

Twisted Log Cabin would be very difficult to make accurately without foundation piecing.

TRY IT

167 Saving fabric

Foundation paper piecing can be quite wasteful of fabric, as you will be cutting out some unusual shapes as you go. Make a set of paper templates from your foundation design (see page 66–67) and use these to cut your fabrics. Give each piece a 3/8-in (10-mm) rather than a 1/4-in (6-mm) seam allowance so you don't get caught short on a seam. Leave the paper template pinned to each patch until you are ready to piece it, so you don't get mixed up.

168 The foundation

Translucent paper foundations allow piecing from the back, because the sewing lines are visible. The stitching perforates the paper so it tears away easily when the piecing is complete. Like foundation piecing stitched from the front (see page 66–67), it is a good technique for tricky fabrics that fray or stretch easily—but being able to follow the design with such precision also means you can achieve more complex patterns. A range of specialized tear-away stabilizer materials is available, but baking parchment or trace also work well. Any crisp, translucent paper that tears off easily could be used. Press your work at each stage for a crisp finish. Use a dry iron, as steam will wrinkle your paper and may smudge ink or pencil marks.

Cutting fabrics with numbered templates will help you organize the patches.

169 Suitable designs

Foundation-pieced patchwork needs a patchwork design that can be assembled by sewing pieces from one end of the block to the other—like a strip of Flying Geese—or from the center outward, like Log Cabin. It is popular for the harder-to-piece Log Cabin variations such as Pineapple Log Cabin, and is essential in order to achieve designs like Twisted Log Cabin with accuracy.

170 Preparing the papers

You can make your papers in various ways, including photocopying onto trace (quick), tracing by hand (slow), or by punching the stitching lines using your sewing machine. For the latter method, pin several layers of foundation paper together with the pattern on top. Unthread your sewing machine and, with an old needle and a fairly short stitch length, "stitch" along all the foundation sewing lines. This will produce multiple copies of the foundation pattern, marked with little perforations. Leave a margin around the edge of each block.

171 **The stitching sequence**

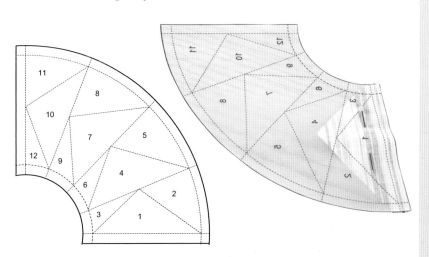

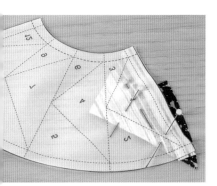

1 | Write the stitching sequence on each paper, as "1," "2," "3," and so on. If you are using a pattern from a book, this information will be there for you to copy. If you are drawing your own pattern, work from the center outward or from one end to the other, as shown in the Flying Geese fan diagram.

2 | Working from the back of the foundation paper, pin the first patch in place with the back of the fabric against the foundation paper, so the section marked "1" is covered and there is at least a ¼-in (6-mm) overlap. Anchor the first strip to the end of the fan shape by stitching within the seam allowance at the end.

3 | Pin the next piece right sides together with the first and check it will cover all the area marked "2" when the seam is sewn along the dashed line. Machine sew the seam using very small stitches, which will help the paper tear away when the piece is complete.

4 | Flip the second patchwork piece over and press it. Now use a pair of scissors to carefully trim away the seam allowance to approximately a ¼ in (6 mm) between the patchwork and the paper. Continue adding the other pieces following the number sequence until the block is complete. Trim the block to match the outer line of the design.

FIX IT

172 *Mirror images*

It can be difficult to remember that you are working from the back and therefore everything is a mirror image. One of the most common problems with non-symmetrical designs is flipping the foundation paper by mistake. Decide at the outset if you want to do this. Being able to read the number sequence on the back of the paper is a help, rather than trying to read mirror images of the numbers through the paper. But if you have flipped the design, remember your fabrics will need to be cut as mirror images too. Using a dyed fabric, either plain or batik, where either side can be used, will avoid this problem, so if you accidentally cut a piece the wrong way round, you can flip the fabric and use the "back."

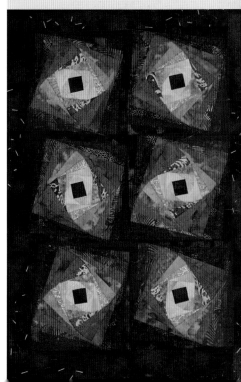

"A black peat stirred, Unsheathed claws like a cat, On the purring hearth" by Catherine Falmer
Foundation-pieced Twisted Log Cabin blocks echo the shape of a cat's claws and flames in this piece from the "Cavalcade of Kings" sequence. Size 30 x 20 in (76 x 51 cm).

Puzzles and weaves

Various "puzzle" and woven effects are made possible by sewing only part of a seam and finishing it after other parts of the patchwork are complete. They are fascinating to look at, and it is usually impossible for others to tell where you started.

TRY IT

173 Using stripes

Using stripes for the rectangles for the Irori block adds a sense of movement. Try stripes to emphasize the woven look, as shown below, or try using one fabric for the vertical strips and another for the horizontal ones.

174 Part-sewn seams

Try out the technique with Irori, a block which copies a feature seen in Japanese architecture and flooring layouts.

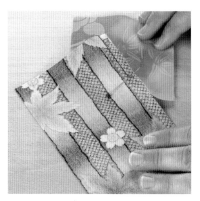

1 | You need a center square and rectangles. The finished size of the rectangles should be the same as the side of the square on the short side and twice the size of the square on the long side. Remember to add ½ in (13 mm) to these measurements to allow for your ¼-in (6-mm) seam allowance.

2 | Place the first rectangle and the square right sides together and line up the two pieces as shown. Machine sew, but only sew half of the seam, as shown in red thread.

3 | Press the seam allowance toward the rectangle, then add the next rectangle. Sew the whole seam this time, then press the seam allowance toward the rectangle again.

4 | Continue until you have added the final rectangle, then complete the first part-sewn seam, overlapping the new stitches with the part-sewn section by at least ½ in (13 mm). Press all the seams toward the outside of the block.

Use this part-sewing technique to make other blocks with woven effects, such as these three modern blocks based on traditional Japanese parquetry designs.

"Kamon Sampler Quilt"
Give a quilt's sashing the woven look on a larger scale, accentuated with shaded fabrics, as shown here; or try using stripes. Size 72 x 68 in (183 x 173 cm).

FIX IT

175 *Don't go too small*

When machine sewing woven effects, a 1-in (25-mm) finished size is the practical minimum for center squares or squares set into the woven patchwork. Any smaller than this and you will not be able to overlap the stitches easily when you complete the first seam, because the back of the machine foot will push into the previous seam allowance.

Inset seams and miters

Where three patchwork seams meet, an inset seam or a miter will be necessary. With a little patience, these are easy to do and look impressive when finished.

FIX IT

176 *Faux miters*

If you like the look of mitered borders but can't get the hang of them, try a faux miter. As with the block below, this works best if the border is pieced from strips arranged at right angles to the edge of the quilt or with striped fabric also arranged at right angles, providing you can use the stripe to hide the extra seam. The corner section is made from a half-square triangle, pieced so the stripes create the miter effect, and the half-square triangle blocks are sewn to the ends of the top and bottom borders before they are sewn to the quilt, avoiding the need for an inset seam.

177 Inset seams

Inset seams are required where three patchwork pieces come together to form a mitered corner. These seams cannot be machine sewn easily in a continuous straight line.

1 | Before you start sewing, mark the seam allowances in the corner points with a dot. Pin the first two pieces together (see page 54).

2 | Sew the first two pieces together between the dots. Start sewing by stitching back toward the dot, then sew between the dots, then reverse stitch again to finish.

3 | Insert the next piece the same way, marking and sewing between the dots. Finally, insert the last piece. Blocks built up using inset seams include T64, T65, and T66. Press all the seams either clockwise or counterclockwise.

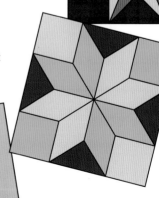

Traditional blocks such as Sunshine and Shadow (top), Star of the East (above), and Attic Windows (left) all require inset seams.

178

Mitered borders

Mitered borders are often avoided by quilters; probably because they are not as economical as borders with butted corners or squares in the corner. But, done well, they can add a stunning frame to your quilt. They are particularly suited to stripes and linear fabric designs, which can be matched in the corners. Add them before layering and quilting.

1 ▎ Decide how wide you want your borders to be and measure the length and width of your quilt (see page 81). Note the measurements for reference. The length of each border should be the length or width of the quilt, plus twice the width of the border, plus an allowance of about 2 in (5 mm) to help you form the miter. Working from the center of the each border strip, mark the

required length for that side. Pin the first border to the edge of the quilt center, being careful not to pin more length of border than the actual length of the side. Join the borders with a ¼-in (6-mm) seam on each side of the quilt, right sides together, making sure you start and stop with a few backstitches a ¼ in (6 mm) from the end of that side. Repeat for each side of the quilt.

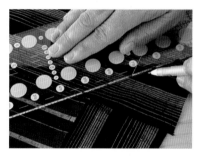

2 ▎ Place the quilt right side down on a flat surface and cross one border over the next. Part of each border strip will overlap and stick out, forming a right angle between them. Draw a straight line from that corner at a 45-degree angle to the inner corner where the border joins the quilt.

3 ▎ Reverse the positions of the borders, and repeat. With the right sides of the borders together, line up the marked seam lines, pin, and stitch from the inner corner to the outer corner.

4 ▎ Open out the corner seam and press it open, checking that any stripes or other pattern motifs are lined up correctly. Press the quilt and border seam toward the border. It should lie neatly from the front.

▦ TRY IT

179 **Multiple strips**

Mitered corners containing multiple strips are a lovely finishing touch. Machine sew strips together to create your borders, making sure you have the strips arranged the same way on each border section, and follow the instructions above, treating your pieced border as if it were a striped piece of fabric.

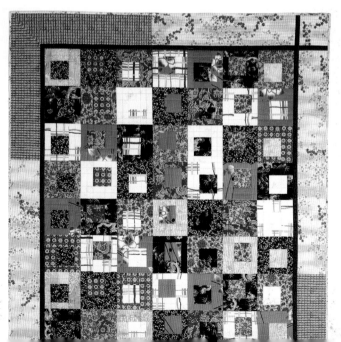

"Chinese Pavilions"
Two border treatments are used in one quilt— diagonally opposite corners have either corner squares or mitered corners using a roof-tile effect print. A dark brown inner strip frames the center patchwork. Size 68 x 56 in (173 x 142 cm).

Curved seams and inset circles

Sewing a curve in patchwork is no more difficult than in dressmaking, except that in this case it needs to lie flat. It is another technique that can add some of the "wow" factor to your quilt.

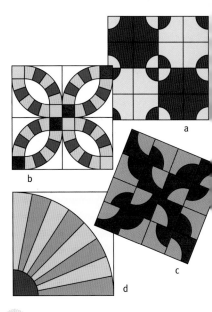

a

b

c

d

180

Cutting curves

Straight lines can be rotary-cut but it is better not to cut tight curves with a rotary cutter—as you turn the cutter around the curve it will slice into your mat and the cut won't heal. Use scissors to cut out curves instead.

1 **|** Cut out the block using three templates: an outer square, an inner segment template, and a fan arc. Pay attention to the direction of the fabric grain and print. The grain on the fans runs at 45 degrees to the grain on the background fabric, so the fabric patterns appear level and realistic on the fans.

181

Blocks with curves

Drunkard's Path (c) is probably the best-known traditional block with curves, but there are many others, including Mill Wheel (a), Double Wedding Ring (b), and Grandmother's Fan (d). Curved piecing is easier than you might think—the bias edges of the fabric are eased together. When you are making your own templates for curves, remember to add a ¼-in (6-mm) seam allowance to the curved part of the template. A fan block is a good choice to practice curved piecing, as it contains both a wide and a tight curve to sew.

2 **|** Fold one fan arc in half and finger-press it. Fold one outer background segment in half and finger-press that too. With right sides together, pin the outer segment to the fan arc, with the fan arc on the bottom, pinning the ends first, with the pins at right angles to the edge. Line up the finger-pressed creases and pin.

3 **|** Now ease the rest of the curved edge together and insert several more pins. Machine sew together, easing the curve as you go. Use a bodkin or large pin to keep the ends of the two pieces together as you sew off the end of the fabric, otherwise they will tend to pull apart. Press toward the background fabric. Sew the inner segment to the block the same way, then repeat for the other blocks.

FIX IT

182 *Sewing curves*

It is usually easier to sew curves with the convex curve below and the concave curve on top. You can ease the two curves together more easily and avoid puckers. If you are still having problems sewing curves—and smaller-scale curved designs can be quite difficult—try a special machine foot for curves, or take the easy option—hand sew the curved seam, as for American patchwork (see page 54).

Piecing a circle

If you can piece a circle segment you can piece a whole circle, setting it into the background fabric. With a little practice, it is quicker than appliquéing a circle. It makes a great background for a traditional Japanese crest, or other designs that benefit from a circular setting, and is an unusual way to frame a feature fabric or scenic design.

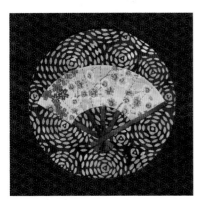

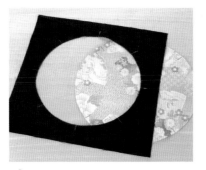

1 ❙ You will need two circle templates, made from card or template plastic. The diameter of the smallest should be 1 in (25 mm) less than the other. One 8-in (203-mm) circle and one 7-in (178-mm) circle template were used for the sample. Draw balance marks around the edge like compass points—north, northeast, east, and so on—on each template. Center the 7-in (178-mm) template on the backing fabric, draw around it, mark the balance marks, and cut out the circle. Mark and cut an 8-in (203-mm) circle from the second fabric.

2 ❙ With the background fabric on top and right sides together, align the balance marks. Pin these points first, then add more pins around the curve. Machine sew the two pieces together, easing around the curve. Remove the pins, open out, and press toward the background (outer) fabric.

"Japanese Fans"
Curved patchwork in these simple 6-in (152-mm) fan blocks adds a lively feeling to a simple stripy quilt, made to showcase the wisteria print in the unpieced strips. Machine quilting adds the fan "sticks." Size 72 x 52 in (183 x 132 cm).

🗌 TRY IT

184 Matching grain lines

If you find piecing curves tricky, try matching the grain line of the two pieces you are sewing together, so when you are sewing a bias edge on one piece, you will be sewing it to the corresponding bias edge on the other. Slightly stretch these bias edges as you sew them together and press flat with a little steam when finished.

Freehand curves

Using the rotary cutter freehand to cut curves is a popular technique used by many contemporary quilters. It works best with gentle, undulating curves.

TRY IT

185 Calming curves

Use the freehand curves to "calm down" optically challenging fabrics, like the black and gold stripes in this detail from the quilt on page 30. Narrow stripes of equal width with strong tonal contrast can seem to shimmer and would be overpowering in a large piece or used with straight piecing.

186 Cutting out curves

A rotary cutter with a smaller blade ($\frac{1}{2}$ in or 1 in/16 mm or 25 mm diameter) is easiest for this technique. Use the reverse of your cutting mat, as the curved cuts won't heal on the surface of the mat. This method gives you two complete strips, with the fabrics in the second one reversed, and almost no wastage.

1 | Cut two 17 x 6 in (432 x 152 mm) pieces of contrasting fabric. Place the fabrics one on top of the other, right sides down, and line up the edges. Use the rotary cutter to carefully cut a gentle curve through both fabric layers. There is no need to use a ruler or guide template. The gentler the curve, the easier it will be to piece!

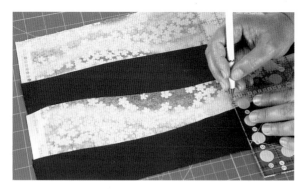

2 | Mark a few balance marks on the curved edge, in the same place on both fabrics. Take the right hand section of one fabric and the left of the other, and place them right sides together.

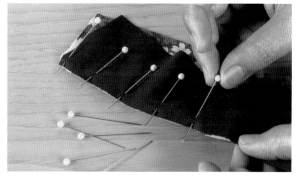

3 | Line up the balance marks and pin the curve at right angles to the edge. As much of the curved edge is on a bias, you will be able to ease one piece of fabric to the other easily. Pin the edges together. Machine stitch with a scant $\frac{1}{4}$-in (6-mm) seam, narrower than the standard one, and press to one side. Press the seam with steam, to ease the fabrics into shape. Cut the piece to the length and width you want.

**"Japanese Sampler"
by Pat Morris**
Another version of the sampler quilt shown on page 30, the freehand curve panels in lilac and green have a minimalist landscape feeling. Colors were coordinated around the fabric featuring a Japanese tea garden. Size 40 x 34 in (102 x 86 cm).

TRY IT

187 Irregular "squares"

Adapt the freehand curve technique by starting with squares of fabric or two fat quarters. Make several freehand cuts across the fabric width and piece the strips to make two panels. Try turning a panel through 90 degrees and cutting with a second piece of one of the same fabrics before piecing the strips together. The resulting pattern will be irregular squareish shapes with wavy edges. Using a plain or small-scale design for the "background" fabric will help disguise the patchwork seams, enhancing the abstract effect.

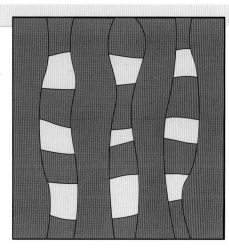

English paper piecing—portable patchwork

A traditional technique, English paper piecing fits remarkably well with modern lifestyles. It is ideal for stitching on the move, on your holidays, at the beach, or simply in front of the television—so you can make use of all those spare moments. It is the easiest way to sew hexagons, diamonds, triangles, and other mitered shapes together.

TRY IT

188 Achieving the impossible!

English paper piecing is the easiest way to piece very complex mosaic designs, involving a lot of set-in seams. A pattern that may seem impossible if pieced any other way can be achieved relatively easily with this method.

189 The speed myth

Many people would dismiss English paper piecing as slow, simply because it is a hand-sewn technique. But because you can use up all those potentially wasted moments to do it, it progresses quickly. It requires little equipment or materials, so it is easy to carry around too. As each piece is basted around a paper template for piecing, there's little chance of making a seam allowance error and some very complex designs are possible, which would be difficult to piece by any other method.

190 Machine appliqué with English paper piecing

If you don't want to make a large piece of English paper-pieced patchwork, you can appliqué single flowers (above) and blocks by hand or machine. Press the patchwork and remove the papers. Pin the patchwork to the background fabric. Machine sew or hand sew around the edge, making sure the seam allowances remain turned under —machine blanket stitch is effective.

"Penrose Tiling" by Pat Storey
English paper piecing was the perfect solution for this complex design, inspired by the maker's mathematical interests. Size 24 in (61 cm) square.

"Hexagon Blues" by Jane Marriott
This patchwork was made while on a round-the-world trip, with fabrics bought in various places. Size 45 x 32 in (114 x 81 cm).

Preparing templates

A good quality template—or accurately cut papers—is essential. A metal template for the shapes you want to use is a good investment, as you will be able to cut all the paper templates you could ever need using this, along with a pair of inexpensive paper scissors (don't ruin your fabric scissors cutting paper templates). Templates are available in various sizes and shapes; buy those that are appropriate for the designs you want to make. Metal templates usually have an outer "window," which you can use to frame up areas of fabric you want to fussy-cut (see page 50).

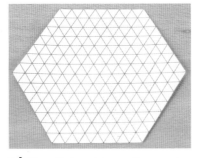

1 **|** To cut papers with a metal template, hold the template tight against the paper and run the scissor blade along the template edge. Many sources of scrap paper are suitable—old brochures and envelopes are ideal, as they are sturdy but not too hard to stitch through. Antique English paper-pieced patchworks occasionally have their papers left in place, revealing reused copy books, letters, envelopes, and other ephemera.

2 **|** Alternatively, cut papers from graph paper. Isometric graph paper is useful for cutting the more popular traditional shapes with 60-degree angles. You can also purchase ready-cut papers. Papers can be reused several times. Cut paper templates to the exact finished size of each piece.

3 **|** Hexagons are the easiest shape, as the 120-degree corner angles mean the seam allowances are neatly tucked in. Baste the fabric patches around the papers, sewing through the paper. The paper dictates the size of the finished patch, so the fabric doesn't have to be cut as precisely as for machine patchwork. Fold the fabric neatly around the paper, finger-pressing the edges by squeezing the fabric over the papers.

4 **|** With right sides together, overcast or whipstitch the pieces together, starting and finishing the sewing with a knot. Begin about ¼ in (6 mm) from the corner of the patch and stitch back toward the corner before proceeding. Don't use very long threads, as hand sewing like this will put a lot of wear on your thread. About 18 in (45 cm) maximum is fine.

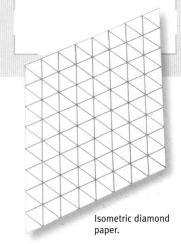

Isometric diamond paper.

5 **|** Insert the next piece in the same way. To keep from handling the patchwork too much while you are sewing, assemble it in sections, and sew the sections together at the end. Press the patchwork when it is complete, and remove the papers. The seam allowances should lie behind their own patch, so the seams remain pressed open, rather than to one side.

Assembling the quilt top

Whether your quilt is made of blocks, single patches or has a one-off asymmetrical design, you will need to join the sections together. Depending on your quilt design, this may involve adding sashing strips, borders, part-sewn seams, or even curved piecing on a large scale for some art quilts. Traditionally, blocks are "set" in various ways (see page 40).

193 Sewing blocks together

Blocks of equal size can be sewn together into strips, pressed, and the strips sewn to each other to make a quilt top, without the need for any extra pieces. Pin blocks carefully and join them neatly. As for sewing blocks, press the seams in opposite directions. If combining patchwork blocks with appliqué, sashiko, or unpieced blocks without seams at the edges, it will be easier to press away from any patchwork blocks used. See Quilt-as-you-go (page 116) for another method for assembling patchwork and quilting in one.

TRY IT

194 Woven sashing

Part-sewn seams (page 70) are used to make sashing with a woven look—the strips appear to go over and under each other in sequence. It is particularly effective with shaded fabrics or stripes. The woven sashing makes joining long strips unnecessary.

If your quilt is not planned using a repeating block layout (above), or uses different sizes of blocks (left), you will need to assemble the top into sections and then sew these together. Make a sketch of the quilt top to help you plan this.

"Tea Things"
The irregular sashing imitates oriental shelves for the appliqué teacups. Size 23 x 16 in (58 x 41 cm).

FIX IT

195 *Different-size blocks*

Use sashing to make blocks of slightly different sizes fit together. It's not unusual for blocks with patchwork pieces in them to finish up as different sizes. It's an especially common problem when blocks are made by more than one person (see page 140). Add a border to each block, then trim them all to the same size. By increasing the size of each block, you'll also make them go further.

Sashing and block borders

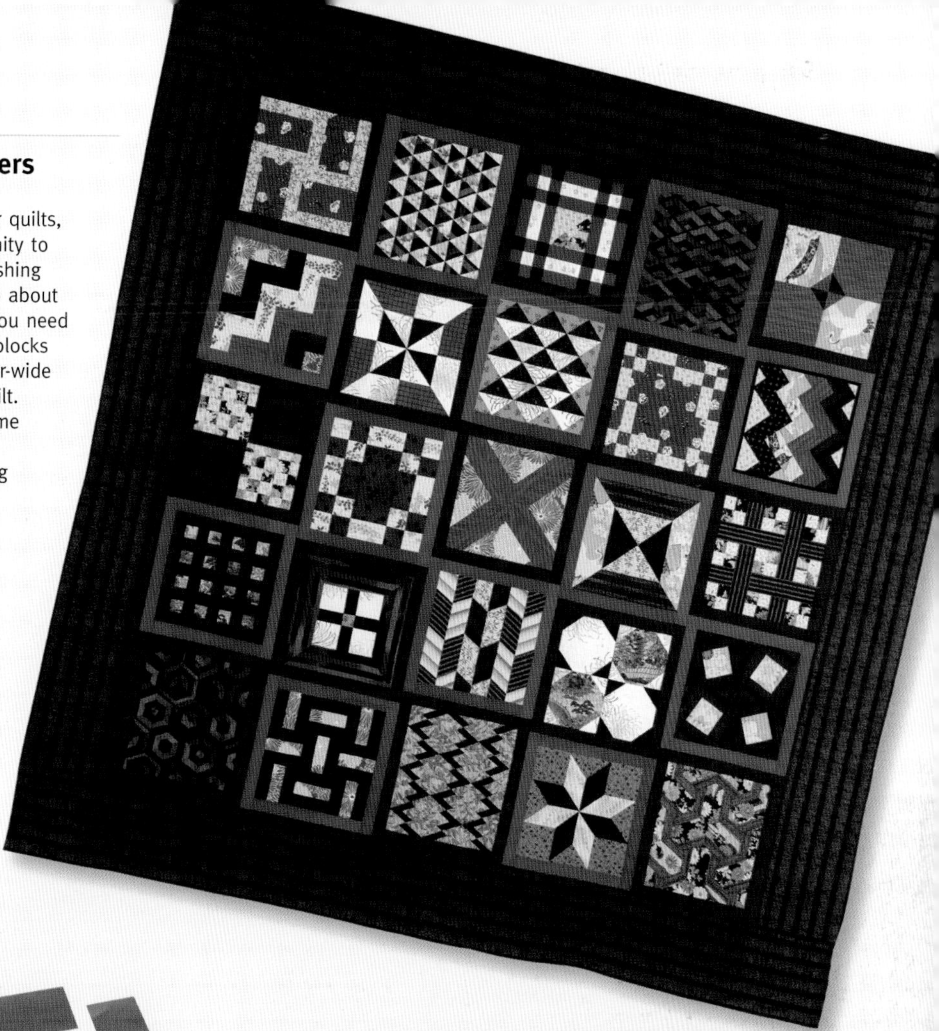

Sashing is especially useful for sampler quilts, such as this one at right, as it gives unity to a large variety of different patterns. Sashing looks in proportion if its width is up to about a quarter of the side of the block—if you need wider sashing, consider bordering the blocks first or adding multiple borders, as over-wide sashing can look odd and spoil the quilt. You can add an outer border in the same way, taking measurements through the center of the quilt top rather than along the edge.

Block borders

For block borders, make the first two borders as long as the side of the block. The next two borders will be longer, equaling the block plus the finished width of the first two borders. If some blocks are slightly smaller or larger than you expected, add borders and trim so all the blocks end up the same size. Pin border strips in place before sewing (see page 56). Press seam allowances between blocks in alternate directions.

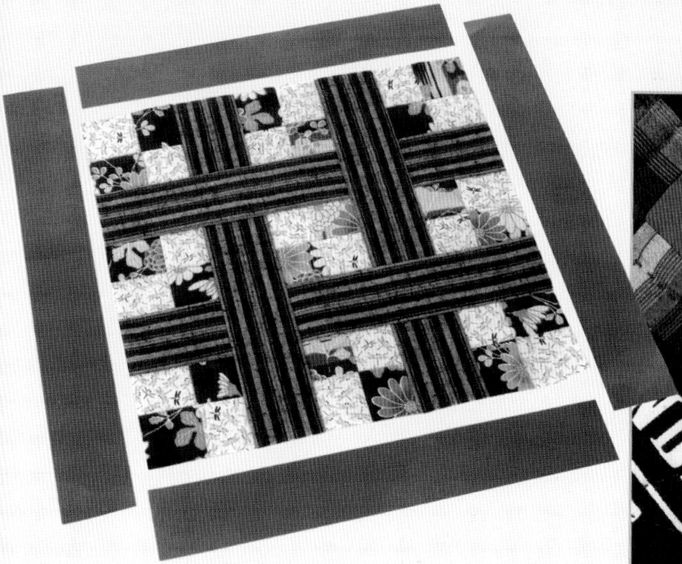

Joining sashing

If you need to cut your sashing from small pieces of fabric, consider using squares, or "posts," to join the strips. With some forward planning, the squares can become part of the design, as shown at right, between "Snowball" blocks.

Japanese folded patchwork

Japanese folded patchwork was devised in the 1980s by Japanese quilter Sachiko Mukari and has become popular worldwide. Fabrics are folded and sewn to form units, usually with batting already inside, which can be hand or machine sewn together to make various designs. No further quilting is needed, which is part of the appeal of this technique.

Firescreen by Gill Young
Japanese folded patchwork hexagons are used as panels for an antique fire screen, coordinated by their red backings. Size 26 x 24 in (66 x 61 cm).

197 Choosing fabrics

Japanese folded patchwork creates a frame effect around the central fabric, which may use fussy cuttings (see page 50) to showcase a particular part of the pattern or a single motif. For versions where the backing fabric is folded over the central patch, fabrics like silk and velvet may be used for the center. Using the same fabric for all the backings—as shown in this screen—helps to unify a large variety of center fabrics in many colors. The backing fabric needs to be folded over a cardboard template and pressed, so patchwork cottons, which hold a crease well, are ideal.

198 Creating hexagons on hexagons

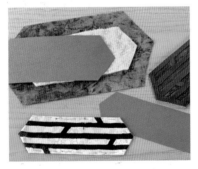

1 | Add the central hexagon last for these layered hexagon units, hiding the raw edges of the larger hexagon backing fabrics. Make the hexagon templates with sides the following lengths—3½ in (8.9 cm) for cutting backing fabric, 2 in (5 cm) for batting and pressing large hexagons, and 1 in (2.5 cm) for pressing smaller center hexagons. For each unit, use the largest template to cut one piece of backing fabric and the middle-size template to cut the batting and the smaller center hexagon.

2 | Using one of the largest fabric pieces and the middle-size template, press the hexagon around the template as shown. Allow the pressed folds to cool, and remove the template. Place a batting piece inside the pressed hexagon and refold the edges. Pin and baste to hold the folds in place.

3 | Fold one of the smaller fabric hexagons around the smallest hexagon template and press. Remove the template. Pin the hexagon to the center of the unit, covering the raw fabric edges and lining up the two hexagons so they are straight. Use a small hemstitch to appliqué the smaller hexagon to the larger one, as shown in step 4, opposite.

FIX IT

Checking the size

Your Japanese folded patchwork units need to be made accurately so they are all the same size and will fit together. Use a template that is the same size as the finished units to check that the size is correct after pinning and before sewing. There is little room for adjustment when sewing the finished units together, so double check while making individual units.

Bag by Maureen Poole
Hand-printed fabrics were created specially for the center hexagons on this Japanese folded patchwork bag and combined with commercial fabrics, with design motifs adapted from traditional half-timbered buildings.

200 Making squares wrapped with circles

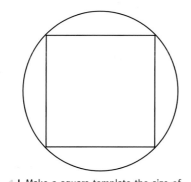

1 | Make a square template the size of your finished unit and a circle template as shown in the diagram. To work out the size of the circle, divide the size of the square by seven and multiply this figure by five—the result is the radius of the circle. For example, a 3½ in (8.9 cm) square needs a circle with a radius of 2½ in (6.4 cm). Make a second circle template of thin card, ¼ in (6 mm) larger all around than the first—½ in (10 mm) larger in diameter. Because the backings will be pressed around these templates with the iron, be careful that ink from recycled card doesn't transfer to your fabric.

2 | Cut squares of feature fabric and batting the same size as your square template. Rotary cutting will be easiest, especially for the batting. Cut circles from your backing fabric with the larger circle template. You will need one square of fabric, one square of batting, and one circle unit. It is easy to work out how many units you need for your project, as they are just squares and you can do it on graph paper. Pin the fabric and batting squares together, as shown.

3 | Sew a line of running stitch around the edge of the first fabric circle, about ⅛ in (3 mm) from the edge. Place the smaller circle template on the wrong side of the fabric circle, and draw up the thread. The hem allowance will be gathered up over the template. Use the tip of a hot iron on the cotton setting to press the hem allowance in place. Be careful not to burn your fingers—an appliqué iron (see page 89) or a travel iron is easiest to use for this. Allow the fabric to cool and the crease to set before removing the template. Repeat for the other circles.

4 | Place the square template on the wrong side of the first fabric circle and press the circle over the pentagon. The circle will form an arc on each edge of the square. Place a fabric and batting square in the center of the fabric circle and fold the circle over the square. The creases you have already ironed will help. Starting on the center of one of the sides, sew the circle to the square, using either a neat hemstitch or small running stitches close to the edge. Add a stitch or two to hold the folds together in each corner. Repeat for the other circles.

APPLIQUÉ AND EMBELLISHMENT TECHNIQUES

Increase your creative repertoire with these techniques,
going beyond patchwork in your quilts.

Appliqué

Appliqué involves laying and stitching one piece of fabric over another to create a
decorative design. It is excellent for pictorial designs and for adding details to patchwork
blocks. Appliqué can be sewn by hand or machine. Fused or bonded appliqué is probably
easiest and is the perfect way to hold fabric in place, prior to machine sewing.

201 Preparing for appliqué

For any appliqué pattern, check the details of the design before
you begin and note where appliqué pieces overlap. Appliqué
patterns from books may need enlarging on a photocopier, if
they have been reduced in size to fit the page. The percentage
increase will be indicated on the pattern. Devise your own
appliqué patterns starting with simple shapes—some of the
techniques on the following pages are more suited than others
to shapes with sharp points or fine indents, so match the
technique you use to the design and its future use. For more
complicated designs, mark the location of each piece lightly on
the background with a fabric marker to help you align them
correctly. There is no need to draw a heavy line around each
shape—a few marks at opposite edges or at the corners of the
appliqué will do.

202 Choosing fabrics

You can have a lot of fun with appliqué fabrics, selecting prints
that are appropriate for your design motif, like the spots for
the black-and-white cat design (see page 86). You don't have to
be too realistic—sometimes a small floral or geometric design
might give the effect you want, such as the tiny floral spots on
the country-style rooster (see page 87). Tone-on-tone prints, like
the yellow floral used for the man-in-the-moon (see page 87),
can help disguise slight shadowing from background prints.

203 Raw-edge appliqué

Hand sew raw-edge appliqué by cutting out
the shape you require, pinning and basting it
to the background fabric, and stitching around
the appliqué with blanket stitch or herringbone
stitch, which will stop the edges fraying. Non-
fraying fabrics, such as felt, can be appliquéd with any
stitch you like, without requiring a hem allowance.
However, materials such as felt are not hardwearing
and it may be best to confine their use to wall hangings
and similar projects. For a machine-stitched version of
this, carefully zigzag over the raw edges (see left). It is best
to cut and pin the appliqué pieces just before sewing them,
to minimize fraying. Ironing the appliqué fabric onto a fusible
interfacing will help to stabilize the appliqué and limit fraying.

204

Featuring raw edges

Appliqué without any edge turning at all can give a soft look to your design if the edge is allowed to fray. Careful choice of fabric and placement of bias edges can emphasize the raw-edge effect. Dyed fabrics rather than prints are more effective for raw-edge techniques. Because the dye goes right through the fabric, the raw edge looks as colorful as the rest of the appliqué, unlike the slightly dulled edge of a raw-edge print. Mark the motif outline on your appliqué fabric and cut out roughly around the appliqué shape. Pin the appliqué to the background fabric. Machine-sew around the appliqué outline once or twice, as desired. Using a pair of sharp scissors, trim away the waste appliqué fabric fairly close to the edge, leaving a little raw edge beyond the stitching line. Appliqué motifs may be added to a panel that is already quilted, as shown below and right.

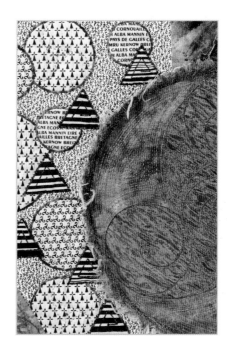

Layered fabrics, allowed to fray heavily at the edges, produce interesting effects. Here, layers of dyed muslin and silk gauze were combined in a large machine-embroidered circle, which was then appliquéd to the background quilt and cut away behind the appliquéd circle. When hung in a window, the circle lights up from behind. A single fabric layer looks effective for the green leaves, shown actual size (far left).

"Timepiece"
A translucent circle in the center of this challenge quilt allows it to be lit from the back as well as the front. Circular motifs cut from the challenge fabric were bonded to make the dense border, with translucent appliqués in gauze and net for the sun's rays and liberal bead embellishment. Size 39⅜ in (100 cm) square.

Fused appliqué

Heat-sensitive bonding is a quick and easy way to attach appliqué pieces. The bonding material also helps to control the appliqué edges and stop them fraying. It is a great technique for crisp, sharp edges with no turning under necessary.

205 Using bonding materials

There are several brands and weights of bonding materials or fusible web that you can iron onto the back of an appliqué piece. Some make a temporary bond, holding the appliqué in place until it is secured by stitching; others form a very strong bond that requires no edge stitching, but makes the fabric very rigid and difficult to sew. All of them enable you to iron the motif you cut out onto ordinary fabric. If you plan to machine sew around the edge, select one that has a medium bond. Check the instructions regarding ironing temperature when you buy the bonding material—if the iron is too cool, it won't bond, but if it is too hot it can burn away the bond. Don't use steam. The iron melts the bonding material, which sticks the appliqué to the backing as it cools. There are also synthetic bonding resins that are shaken onto the fabric in tiny granules.

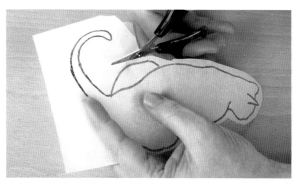

Make appliqué easy by ironing the bonding material to the back of your fabric before cutting out the pieces. This way the bond will go all the way to the edge of your appliqué piece, helping prevent fraying. Begin by tracing the pattern pieces onto the paper backing, remembering to draw a mirror image of the pattern. Roughly cut around the piece.

206 Ironing on bonding

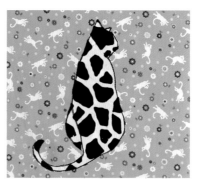

1 | Following the manufacturer's instructions, iron the web onto the back of your fabric. Use a pressing cloth or nonstick pressing sheet between your work and the iron to prevent the iron soleplate getting covered in sticky, burned-on plastic fibers from the bonding material. When the piece has cooled, carefully cut around the appliqué shape. Transfer any detail lines onto the fabric, by tracing through against a lightbox, backlit window, or similar.

2 | Peel off the paper backing, position the appliqué on your background fabric, and press—again, following the manufacturer's instructions and using a pressing cloth or sheet to protect your work. If there is more than one piece to appliqué, iron on the next piece in order. Machine stitch around the motif and add details such as eyes, feathers, and so on for animals and birds.

TRY IT

207 Different edging stitches

Try different stitches to edge your appliqué to vary the effect produced. An appliqué foot for the machine, either with an open "toe" or a slightly raised plastic front, will enable you to see where you are stitching and keep the stitches from bunching up under the foot. Loosen the top thread tension slightly, so the bobbin thread isn't pulled up at the sides of the stitch.

Running stitch

Three or four parallel lines of running stitch allow for plenty of detail and give a sharp, defined edge but with a hint of softness—good for fur and feathers. It doesn't matter if the stitch lines cross. Select a thread color that will make the appliqué stand out from the background and show any necessary details. Variegated threads make the outline appear softer.

Satin stitch

Satin stitch (machine zigzag with a short stitch-length) gives a heavier, solid edge. You will need to match your thread carefully, and avoid using mostly dark threads unless you want a cartoon effect. Machine embroidery threads (finer 60s threads) and a needle with a sharp point, like a Microtex or even a fine denim needle, will help produce a clean zigzag satin stitch, with a sharp turn at either side of the stitch. A universal needle will make the ends of the stitch more of a "U"- than a "V"-shape.

Machine blanket stitch

Machine blanket stitch gives blocks a folk-art look. Use a contrasting color for the blanket stitch, to make the stitches stand out. Sometimes a thread that looks bright and quite overpowering on the reel will give just enough color to an appliqué edge to help "lift" it from the background. This panel combines an English paper-pieced flower in machine appliqué over a bonded flowerpot and leaf—the hexagon flower isn't bonded.

FIX IT

208 *Appliqué problems*

THE RIGHT ORDER Make sure you get the order right when appliquéing multiple pieces in one design. For example, the man in the moon's face (see left) was ironed on first, then his nightcap, and finally the tassel. The cap overlaps his face by about 1/8 in (3 mm). All the stitching was added after the bonding was complete. Keep a picture of the appliqué to hand to help you layer the pieces in the right order.

JUST ENOUGH LAYERS Ironing too many layers can cause various problems—your work will either become stiff with too many layers of bonding web (some are plastic adhesives) or some of the initial layers may begin to lift off while you are adding the last few. A good appliqué design won't have unnecessary layers of fabric. Try not to iron over sections that have already been bonded too many times.

USE STABILIZER Zigzag machine appliqué stitches, particularly satin stitch and blanket stitch, have a tendency to "tunnel"—the fabric is lifted up to form a slight ridge. Whether or not this happens depends on several factors, including the type of machine foot you are using and the thread tension, but can be easily fixed by placing a sheet of tear-away stabilizer underneath the appliqué as you sew. This can be as simple as a sheet of baking parchment, or you can use a special stabilizer made for appliqué. Simply tear it away when you have finished stitching.

Freezer paper appliqué

This modern appliqué method uses paper templates behind the fabric. The fabric is then folded and pressed over the paper edge precisely following it, so its shape is precisely the same as the shape of the paper. The appliqué can then be sewn by hand or by machine.

209 Freezer paper and its substitutes

Freezer paper was originally intended as a food wrapping. It has a waxy side that will stick to the back of fabric when it is heated with a dry iron. Freezer paper for kitchen use is supplied as a roll and can now be bought in quilt shops. It is also made especially for quilters in A4 or letter—8½ x 11 in (21.6 x 27.9 cm)—size sheets, which can be printed on using a photocopier or computer; so you can easily make multiple copies of a repeat appliqué pattern. If you cannot buy freezer paper, substitute waxy wrappers from photocopier papers.

FIX IT

211 *Removing the paper*

Removing the paper can be tricky if pieces are small or thin and you only want to slit the background fabric, not trim it away. A pair of tweezers can help you get hold of the paper and remove it from narrow spaces. If some of the pieces will be just too small to allow you to remove the paper easily, iron the freezer paper to the front of the appliqué rather than the back and use the edge of the paper to help you needleturn the turning allowance under (see page 90).

210 Preparing appliqué pieces

Prepare your pattern on the non-waxy side of the freezer paper, by tracing, photocopying, or printing. If you want to iron the waxy side of the paper to the back of your fabric, make sure the pattern is a mirror image of the finished design. If you want initially to pin the freezer paper to your fabric and use the waxy side to hold the fabric edges folded in place and stick the appliqué temporarily to the background, the pattern should end up the right way around on the paper instead.

Method: Cut out your pattern pieces from the freezer paper and iron each one to the back of the fabric, sticking the template in place. Cut the fabric out after the template has cooled, leaving a ¼ in (6 mm) turning allowance. Turn the fabric edges under, crisply, against the edge of the template and press them in place, clipping around curves as necessary. Where the edge of an appliqué piece will be covered by the next piece, there is no need to turn that edge under. Pin the appliqué to the background fabric or stick the freezer paper temporarily with a dab of fabric glue.

212 Sewing by machine

Set your machine either to a very small zigzag or to machine hemstitch—the machine takes several straight stitches, then a single zigzag and repeats this. The stitches should be set short and narrow. Use invisible machine sewing thread for completely invisible stitches. Polyester invisible thread is softer than nylon monofilament. Take care not to melt synthetic appliqué threads when you lightly press your finished work. Stitch around the appliqué piece, so one part of the zigzag goes into the backing fabric and the other into the appliqué. If using the machine hemstitch, the straight stitches should be in the backing fabric only, as close as possible to the edge. An appliqué foot will help you see where you are stitching, either with an open toe or a clear plastic foot.

213 Sewing by hand

Hand-sew the piece with the edge of the appliqué toward you, so you can see your stitches. Come up through the edge of the appliqué shape, catching just a few fabric threads, and down through the backing fabric, so the appliqué is pulled down against the backing fabric as you tighten each stitch. Keep your stitches at right angles to the edge, so the stitches on top of the appliqué are straight. If you allow the stitches to slant, they will immediately cease to be invisible! Stitches should be about $\frac{1}{16}$–$\frac{1}{8}$ in (2–3 mm) apart. Try not to stitch through the edge of the paper, so it can be removed easily later.

214 Finishing the appliqué

After sewing the appliqué, use a pair of fine appliqué scissors or pointed embroidery scissors to cut away the background fabric behind the appliqué. Pull the backing fabric away from the appliqué slightly as you start and be careful not to cut the appliqué. Leave a $\frac{1}{4}$ in (6 mm) overlap, and gently pull the paper out. If you would prefer to leave the fabric in place, simply cut a slit in the backing fabric and pull the paper out through that. Lightly press the finished appliqué, being careful not to squash the appliqué hard against the background, which will spoil the finished effect.

🔲 TRY IT

215 Using the right tools

Products made specially for appliqué will help to make your work easier. Appliqué threads are finer than 50s threads used for patchwork, including 60s and 100s threads. Fine silk threads for hand appliqué are virtually invisible in use, and a small selection of neutral shades will blend with all your fabrics. A small travel iron is easier to use to press the turning allowances under. Better still, a specialist appliqué iron has a very small plate on the end of a wand, enabling precise work without roasting your fingers. The plate can be covered with a non-stick material to stop it sticking to freezer paper or bonding materials.

A detail from the "November" quilt.

"November"
Autumn leaves were collected, pressed, and dried between sheets of newspaper, and used to make the freezer paper templates for this quilt, for a natural effect. Hand-appliquéd leaves with veins were hand embroidered in stem stitch. Size 80 in (203 cm) square.

Needleturn and reverse appliqué

Also known as "template-free appliqué" (although you can use templates), needleturn appliqué gives a firm, strong edge to the appliquéd shape. With a little practice, needleturn is a quick and portable appliqué method because there are few steps and no machine sewing— no pressing is required in advance. It is the easiest way to stitch reverse appliqué.

FIX IT

216 *Corners not sharp enough?*

• Points, corners, and indents should be as sharp as possible. Achieve sharp points and corners by leaving the last couple of stitches loose, pushing the point of the fabric under the shape as far as possible (see below), and then gently tightening the sewing thread. The loose stitches will tighten up and the point will pull out perfectly. Add an extra stitch at the point.
• Clip fabric at the corner of indented sections, but avoid very narrow indents in any appliqué design that requires a turning allowance—narrow indents simply won't have enough fabric to turn under for the hem. Place appliqué stitches more closely together around indented points.

217

The basic method

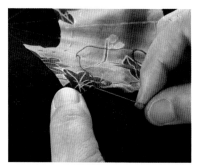

1 | Cut out your appliqué pieces, with a ⅛ in (3 mm) turning allowance all around. Abstract shapes can be cut freehand—practice with paper first. For more detailed appliqué, you will want to use paper templates, which can simply be pinned to the front of your fabric for cutting out. Baste the appliqué piece to the background fabric, with small stitches ¼ in (6 mm) from the cut edge, as shown. The basting stitches prevent too much fabric being turned under. Where the edge of an appliqué piece will be covered by the next piece, there is no need to turn that edge under.

2 | Use an appliqué needle or a long sharp to turn under the turning allowance, using the point to stroke it into place. Hand-sew with the edge of the appliqué toward you. Come up through the edge of the appliqué, catching a few fabric threads, and down through the backing fabric, pulling the appliqué down against the fabric. Keep your stitches at right angles to the edge and about ¹⁄₁₆–⅛ in (2–3 mm) apart. It is not necessary to clip the fabric on a curve; just ease it under. Only clip into deep "V" shapes. Start and finish on a long side.

218

Creating an illusion of depth

Use reverse appliqué to create an illusion that one object is behind another, where the background fabric might shadow through the turning allowance at the edge of the appliqué, where the motif fabric is thick or frays readily, or when it is simply easier to achieve a narrow design that way. The appliqué motif fabric is visible through a hole cut in the main fabric (in ordinary appliqué, this would be the background).
Method: Mark your cutting lines on the main fabric, which is now going to be placed on top of the motif fabric and pinned to it. The motif fabric needs to overlap the motif area by at least ½ in (13 mm) all around. Tack the fabrics together, stitching ⅛ in (3 mm) away from the cutting lines, on the outside of the motif. Using a small, sharp pair of scissors, carefully cut away the top fabric to reveal the motif fabric, cutting ⅛ in (3 mm) away from the marked line, as shown. Needleturn appliqué the edge. Further layers can then be added and appliquéd. For a machine version of reverse appliqué, machine sew close to the marked line after pinning, just inside where the edge will be cut, trim away the top fabric, and machine satin stitch over the previous stitches and the raw edge.

"Zen—Garden from the Tea House"
Although all the appliquéd maple leaves are the same
size, individual leaf color and position tell the viewer that
one is drifting into the tearoom, while the others are outside. Note
how appliquéing the top edge of the green fabric over the brown,
but the lower edge under the brown gives
the illusion that the green "tea" is
in the bowl. Size 37 x 25 in
(94 x 64 cm).

TRY IT

219 Appliqué illusions

A few simple fabric selection tricks will enhance your
appliqué designs:
• Choose fabric that hints at the effect you want to
achieve, like the striped fabrics for the arrow feathers on
the Japanese kamon (family crest) design (below right).
• Cutting parts of the appliqué from one piece of fabric,
so the pattern passes from one part of the appliqué to
another, gives an interesting effect. For instance, the
cherry blossom is centered on a flower in the print,
which looks like the center of the blossom (below center).
• Accent your appliqué with embroidered details in
running stitch, stem stitch, French knots, or other
stitches. The butterfly antennae are in stem stitch, with
French knots at the ends (below left).
• For pictorial designs, consider various effects, such
as size and elevation—larger motifs will appear closer;
objects that are higher up will seem farther away. If
two objects overlap, the overlapped object will
seem farther away too. Use color and
tone effects to enhance depth
in the design (see Color
for perspective,
page 31).

Hawaiian appliqué

The elaborate, large-scale patterns that are characteristic of Hawaiian appliqué begin as paper cuts, although, with experience, you might cut them direct from your fabric. Plain red or blue on white are traditional colorways, but other combinations are also popular today.

FIX IT

220 *Having trouble placing pieces accurately?*

Take care when pinning the appliqué fabric to the background, that the edges of motifs don't become overlapped or long, thin sections of the appliqué become distorted or out of alignment. You can check that the appliqué is correctly laid out after pinning by placing the leftover fabric on top of the appliqué and making sure the cut edges line up.

221

Designing your pattern

You can cut a unique Hawaiian appliqué pattern from folded paper, so the images mirror and repeat from the quilt center, just like they will on the appliqué fabric. Individuality is highly prized among Hawaiian quilters and it would be a major *faux pas* or even bad luck to copy another quilter's design (fortunately, this rule does not apply to published patterns). Experiment with designs before you cut your fabric. Similar but simplified folded repeat designs are seen in some American appliqué quilts, including nineteenth century quilts made by the Pennsylvanian German immigrant community and some "Baltimore Beauty" appliqué samplers, which probably links the designs to northern European paper cutting or scherenschnitte traditions. A small design is a good place to start.

1 | Take an 18 in (47.7 cm) square of paper and fold it in half, then into quarters, and then in half again to make a triangular shape. Traditional designs are based on this eighth fold, but you may like to experiment with a quarter fold or even folding into sixths, for a hexagonal design.

2 | Sketch your design on one section of the folded paper. You need to keep the design linked together, so use branches and stems in your design. Narrow indents and points are difficult to appliqué as there will be little hem allowance to turn under. Cut half of a flower or leaf on a fold line for symmetrical motifs.

3 | Open out the paper. You will have a paper version of a pattern with a symmetrical design. Keep making patterns until you are happy with the result. You need only one "eighth" of a segment of the pattern to cut your fabric.

222

Perfect cutting

Fold the fabric into eighths, as you did with the paper when making the pattern, and press the creases for accuracy. Pin an "eighth" segment of the pattern to your fabric. Be generous with your pins, and make sure you are pinning through all eight layers. Cut out the appliqué with a pair of sharp scissors, as you will be cutting through eight layers, and cut ⅛ in (3 mm) away from the edge of the paper pattern, so you add the appliqué turning allowance onto the fabric. You should be able to cut the fabric so the leftover piece comes away in one piece—you could use this to make a reverse version of the design. Any cutout sections that are completely enclosed by the appliqué design will be separate pieces of course. Open out the appliqué fabric.

223

Placing and sewing

You need to line up the patterns accurately before you begin basting, which can be tricky on larger projects. The appliqué fabric will have creases along the fold lines. Fold and press the background fabric the same way. Pin the design to the background, without stretching fabric, lining up the pressed folds. Baste the appliqué as for needleturn appliqué (page 90). Keep the fabrics smooth and wrinkle-free. Remove the pins and stitch the appliqué using the needleturn method on page 90.

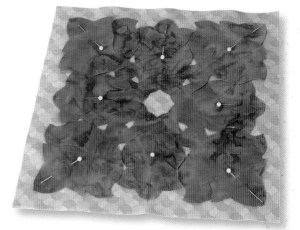

🔲 TRY IT

224 **Five tips for quilting for maximum effect**

The quilting materials and technique are important to the overall effect.
• Polyester batting will fill the appliqué nicely and make the design puffier than if cotton batting is used (see page 104).
• Plain fabric for the quilt backing will show off the quilting when the quilt is seen from the back.
• Echo quilting, in which the lines appear to ripple outward from the appliqué, is stitched in radiating lines, starting at the appliqué edge.
• Use the width of your finger as an easy guide for spacing the lines in traditional style, so you don't need to mark the quilting lines (or remove them later).
• Quilt one line out from the center for each line out from the border. Where the inner and outer quilting lines eventually meet, fill in the spaces between by echo quilting around the shape, in ever-decreasing outlines. Quilt "in the ditch" along the edge of each appliqué shape.

You can add details, such as leaf veins, to parts of the appliqué, or add a line of echo quilting inside the design.

Bias strips appliqué

Bias strips are perfect for fine linear designs like flower stems and Celtic patterns. You can use ready-made fusible bias strips or make your own and stitch them in place.

225 Marking bias tape designs

Trace guidelines for bias tape designs onto your backing fabric, using a quilting pencil. If your tape width is the same as the lines in the design, draw a line on either side, so you will be able to position the tape easily. If the line width and tape width differ, draw lines along the center of the design lines, where it will be hidden by the tape. Where lines cross as part of the pattern, make a break in the line you are drawing, so you know where the bias tape will overlap. Use these overlapping points in the pattern to hide the ends of bias strips, tucking them under the upper strip as it crosses the join.

226 Fusible bias appliqué

Ready-made fusible bias strips (a Japanese product) are easiest to use to represent stems, ribbons, branches, and so on. Following the manufacturer's instructions, iron them on and stitch in place with small stitches, as for needleturn appliqué (see page 90). Alternatively, machine stitch in place, either with a tiny zigzag or using a twin needle slightly narrower than the tape width. Bias tape makers are available to make tape in various widths, and you can buy the iron-on adhesive strips to complete your homemade tape, so you can make tape to match other fabrics in your design.

FIX IT

227 *Choosing the right iron*

To avoid burned fingers, a mini iron has a small sole-plate at the end of a wand and is ideal for ironing tape onto backing fabric, or use a travel iron.

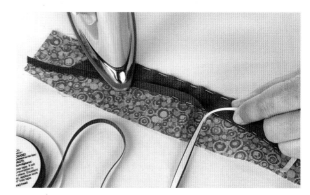

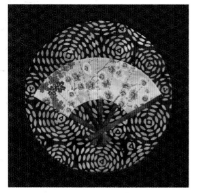

Fusible effects
Fusible bias tape was used for the "sticks" on the fan design above, with the ends tucked under the fan "paper" or folded under and stitched.

Dealing with edges
Where the bias tape will overlap the edge of a shape in the design, simply baste the shape and cover the raw edge with the bias strip. The various colors included on the shaded tape make matching almost any color possible. Take care not to overstretch the outside of the tape on a tight curve.

Architectural details
Bias tape is useful for architectural details, as on this Japanese torii gate block. It is used to cover over the raw edge at the top of the gate where the tape ends go into the seam allowance around the block. For the narrow gate bar, the tape ends were folded back under the tape and stitched in place.

228 Using a pressing sheet

A translucent sheet made from non-stick, heat-resistant material is useful for assembling complicated Celtic knotwork patterns using fusible bias tape. Position the pressing sheet over the knotwork drawing and use a mini iron to fix the tape to the sheet. Where the tapelines cross, iron the upper tape to the lower one. These crossing points hold the appliqué tape motif in place, so this method is not suitable for any design where the tape doesn't cross. When the design is complete and cooled, it can be peeled from the sheet and ironed onto the background fabric.

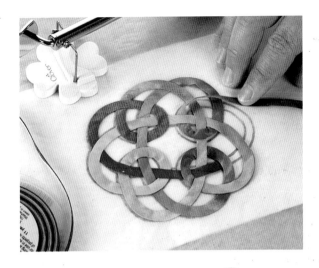

229 Making bias tape for stitching

Another way to deal with bias tape designs is to make your own stitched bias tubes and press the seam allowance to the back using a pressing bar. Made from heat-resistant plastic, the pressing bar is also used as a guide to sewing the tubes.

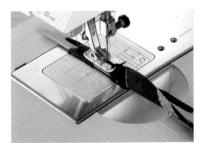 

1 | Cut bias strips to the required width for the bar you wish to use—this will be wider than the bar. Although you only need an ⅛ in (3 mm) seam allowance, this can be tricky to sew for narrow tubes, so allow a ¼ in (6 mm) seam allowance on either side of the strip, adding ½ in (13 mm) to the finished width of the bias strip, and trim the seam allowance after sewing. Fold the strips in half lengthwise, wrong sides together, and press. Machine-stitch 2 in (5 cm), allowing just enough space in the fabric tube for the bias bar. Raise the presser foot and slide the bar into the tube to check the width. If it is too narrow, make the seam allowance smaller; too wide, make it larger.

2 | Sew the rest of the seam. Trim the seam allowance to measure approximately ⅛ in (3 mm). Slide the pressing bar inside the tube. Twist the tube and bar until the seam and seam allowances are on one side of the bar, without sticking out on either side. Press the seam to lie in one direction, moving the pressing bar through the tube until the bar comes out the other end. Repeat for each tube. To use the bias tubes, pin and baste them to the background fabric and hand sew the edges in place, using the same stitch as freezer paper and needleturn appliqué methods on pages 88 and 90.

"Brown Owl" by Maureen Poole
A bold design like this owl is perfect for stained glass appliqué. The bias tape is hand appliquéd over the vest.

230 Stained glass appliqué

Stained glass appliqué is suited to bold designs that can be outlined in the style of stained glass. Mark your design onto a calico backing. Cut out the individual appliqué pieces without any seam allowances and fit them together like a jigsaw on the backing, lining them up with the marked pattern. Pin and baste. Apply bias tape overlapping the raw edges, using whichever tape method you prefer. For even easier stained glass appliqué, fuse the appliqué pieces to the backing (see fused appliqué, page 86).

Broderie persé and shadow appliqué

Also known as appliqué persé, broderie persé began as a method of making expensive chintzes go further, by cutting out the motifs and appliquéing them to a plain background. Shadow appliqué is overlaid with a sheer fabric, producing a misty effect. Both are traditional techniques that can be used for a contemporary look.

TRY IT

231 Metallic outlines

Machine outlining with metallic thread looks effective. Change to the metallica needle and thread your machine with metallic thread of your choice. Slightly loosen the top tension and use gold-colored thread in the bobbin. Metallic threads create greater friction and heat as they run through the thread guides and tension disks, so go slowly. If the thread shreds, go slower. If it continues to shred, change to a new needle. Metallica needles have a specially designed eye to help the thread run without quickly wearing a groove in the needle, which would cause the thread to shred, but they still require changing more frequently than ordinary needles. Stitch slightly to the outside of the motif, rather than directly on top of any outline.

232 Choosing fabrics for broderie persé

Look for fabrics with bold, clear motifs, such as the one shown at right, that you can cut out and appliqué. Simple edges are easiest to work with for hand appliqué, which can be needleturned (see page 90). More elaborate motif edges are best dealt with by machine appliqué. Look for contrast with your background fabric. Clusters of motifs or individual motifs can be used, for example making a flower bouquet out of individual floral motifs. If your chosen motif is partially obscured by another, don't discard the idea: think about overlapping the part you don't want to see with another motif. You may also like to prepare a machine-quilted panel on which to work broderie persé.

233 Broderie persé by machine

1 | For machine appliqué, cut roughly around the motifs, taking care not to chop through other parts of the print that you want to use, and leaving about ¼ in (6 mm) extra fabric all round. Arrange your motifs on the background and pin them in place. Place a tear-away stabilizer under your work to reduce the risk of puckering. Using the quilting foot and dropped feed dogs, stitch around the outline of the motif.

2 | When the motif is complete, use embroidery scissors to trim away excess fabric. Where a small area of background is enclosed by the motif, it may be necessary to leave it in place, such as the black sections behind the wisteria flowers on the lilac cushion. Larger areas can be trimmed away—hold the waste fabric away from the quilted surface with the point of a pin before making the first cut.

235

Broderie persé by hand

For hand appliqué, cut out motifs with a ⅛ in (3 mm) turning allowance all around. Arrange the motifs on your panel. Baste the motif to the background and appliqué, following the instructions for needleturn appliqué on page 90. Appliqué motifs can be combined in interesting ways with patchwork, allowing a motif from the patchwork fabric to drift across seam lines.

Individual appliquéd blossoms are embellished with beads.

236

Shadow appliqué

In this technique, also known as shadow quilting, appliqué pieces are sandwiched between the background fabric and a sheer top layer, which may be organza, chiffon, silk, nylon gauze, or any other semitransparent fabric. It must be sufficiently transparent to allow the design to show through while also obscuring the appliqué pieces, giving a "misty" or moiré effect. You'll need a strong contrast between the background and the appliqué. The appliqué is held in place by stitching closely around each piece but you may also like to secure the pieces by bonding them to the background first (see page 86).
Method: Cut out the appliqué shapes and stick them to the background with fabric glue (if you are not bonding them), arranging them as you wish. Smooth the sheer fabric over the top of the appliqué and pin closely around the design. Select thread that blends with the top fabric and stitch around the appliqué—in effect, quilting through just two layers.

"Shadow panel" by Barbara Howell
This simple but bold shadow appliqué picture gives a contemporary look to an ancient Celtic motif.

The appliqué in this quilted picture is cut from fleece fabric for a three-dimensional effect. Felt would also work well. Nylon fibers were laid loosely across the appliqué before the top fabric was layered, adding to the shimmering effect.

Embellishments

Almost anything that can be stitched or stuck to the surface of fabric can be used as a quilting embellishment —buttons, beads, ribbon, lace, and much more. There are almost no limits.

237 Where to embellish

Most embellishments are added after quilting, although ribbon, lace, and flat braids (below) may be sewn into the patchwork, securing the ends in the seams. Study your quilt design and decide what kind of embellishments might be suitable and where you want to use them. Quilts that are randomly plastered with unrelated embellishments lack unity in their design, so consider what kind of embellishment you want to use and where you can apply it to highlight the design. For example, you may decide that sparkly narrow cord couched around appliqué motifs and in the ditch around the patchwork might be best for a wall hanging with metallic quilting and appliqué threads, along with some metallic beads.

238 Planning embellishments

Consider the eventual use of your quilt when planning any embellishments. Lumpy embellishments, such as large buttons, won't be comfortable to sit on for a sofa throw. The extra softness of a cushion pad makes embellishments less of a problem, although you would want to avoid embellishments that might become caught on clothing. Any embellishments that can be pulled off, like buttons and beads, should not be used for a young child's quilt, but would be acceptable for a quilt kept out of reach on a nursery wall.

239 Featuring ribbon, braid, lace, and cords

Ribbon can be appliquéd flat, in a similar way to bias tape (see page 94), but is best for straight lines because its straight weave is difficult to bend around curves. It can also be used to make bows and rosettes. Silk ribbon will hold a knot more readily than polyester ribbon, and can be bought in many colors, including hand-dyed effects, for silk-ribbon embroidery. Velvet ribbons, appliquéd flat to your design, add a change of texture. Sew ribbons by hand or machine. Take care if you need to press an area near synthetic ribbon, keeping the iron cool so you don't melt it.

Badges are the quickest embellishment.

Braid adds texture and can be purchased in a wide variety of widths and colors. Some heavily textured braids are easiest to sew by hand, while others can be applied by machine. Study the structure of the braid to find unobtrusive places to sew through, where your stitches will be hidden. Wide braids make good borders and decorative details for patchwork bags. Some braids are so ornate you could theme a project around them. Cords can be couched, by hand or machine, used to outline features or make knotwork designs. Braids and cords usually contain synthetic fibers, often nylon and rayon, so take care if pressing.

Lace, old or new, adds a pretty touch. It can be applied by hand or machine. Vintage lace is best reserved for items that won't get a lot of wear. More robust modern laces may be machine-washed. Press lightly with a cool iron.

Very thick threads and cords can be couched by hand or machine. A cording foot has a hole at the front to feed the thread, keeping it in place as it is machine stitched. Thick threads can also be couched from below, used in the machine bobbin. Some manufacturers sell a special bobbin case for "embroidery" threads; alternatively you will need to loosen your bobbin tension.

Pretty trims for embellishing a quilt project.

240 Adding buttons, badges, and baubles

Buttons can give an antique or country look, depending on the style and material. Novelty buttons are made with all kinds of motifs, such as little flowers. Buttons are best added after quilting, as they are tricky to quilt around.

Badges are a very quick form of embellishment and can be removed for washing.

Look out for costume jewelry and worn-out clothing with pretty buttons as they provide sources for embellishment and may suggest a theme for your project.

"Crazy Embellishments"
by Jenny Hewer
Dozens of different embellishments are used. Size 18 in (46 cm) square.

FIX IT

241 *Washing dilemmas*

Some embellishments can't be washed easily, so check for washability before you apply them to a project that will need to be washed. Non-washable embellishments are best kept for wallhangings, unless they are items you can temporarily remove, like badges. It is wise to preshrink braids and lace by soaking them in warm water first. Try a test wash for colorfastness before hand couching long lengths of braid. Hand wash items decorated with buttons and beads, which may break in a washing machine.

TRY IT

242 Unusual embellishments

There are lots of items for scrapbooking, cardmaking, and embroidery that are robust enough for use on quilted items, including braids, eyelets, and charms. Keep your eyes open for other sources—the silver snowflake below was a wineglass charm.

Crazy patchwork

Crazy patchwork is a Victorian technique that is still very popular, and is actually a type of appliqué. Scraps of fabric, ribbon, and lace are stitched onto a foundation fabric and embellished with embroidery stitches, buttons, and beads, for a rich and textured effect.

FIX IT

244 *Crazy patchwork looking a bit too crazy?*

Scraps used for crazy patchwork can be all kinds of fabrics, textures, and colors, and a piece can begin to look disorganized and uncoordinated. Using the same thread for all your edge stitching or even the same stitch throughout will help to restore unity to your work. Leave embellishments like buttons, beads, and sequins until the end, as you can use these to balance the design visually. If there are one or two patches that really don't work and detract from the patchwork, you can always appliqué another patch over them and hide them completely!

Yellow perlé thread unifies this patchwork bag.

243

Choosing fabrics and embellishments

Because the foundation fabric does the job of supporting everything, different kinds of fabrics can be combined, such as silks and velvets (see page 18). Irregular pieces can be included, so crazy patchwork is an ideal technique for using up the odd-shaped scraps left over from cutting out appliqué pieces.

Wide ribbon can be used like fabric, while narrower ribbon, braid, or lace can be laid over crazy patchwork pieces. Overlap the edges of fabrics that fray easily—such as velvet—with other pieces of material, and treat raw ends of ribbons, braid, and lace the same way. You can color-coordinate your crazy patchwork or go for a random effect. Victorian crazy patchwork was made when silk and velvet were popular dressmaking fabrics and this is reflected in antique pieces, so use these fabrics if you want an old-fashioned look.

245

Making crazy patchwork

There are two main ways to make crazy patchwork—as a random appliqué or as units of stitch-and-flip patchwork. The appliqué method can be worked with raw edges or with a small hem allowance. Whichever method you use, you will need a backing panel slightly larger than the finished piece. Plain cotton calico is ideal for this.

1 | For the appliqué method, you can start anywhere you like on the panel, but you will want to position fabrics that fray and are too thick to turn under easily, like velvet, where they can be overlapped by other fabrics. Pin the first piece in place and hand stitch to the backing around the edge of the patch, close to the edge.

2 | Take another scrap that will overlap the edge of the first one and press one edge under. Pin it to the backing, overlapping one edge of the first piece by about ¼ in (6 mm) and appliqué in place, stitching the folded edge as for appliqué (see page 84), and using running stitch for the rest of the patch. Continue adding more patches, incorporating lace, ribbon, and braid, so the ends are hidden. Occasionally you will need to have a turning allowance on more than one side, if you are filling in a gap between two patches. Continue until the backing is covered with patches.

Crazy patchwork by machine

Crazy patchwork can be made with raw edges if sewn by machine, using a decorative machine stitch to finish off the edges as each patch is sewn in place, rather than leaving the decorative edge finishes to the end as with the hand-sewn method.

Method: This circular bag panel was started at the outer edge, with striped cotton rectangles and wedge shapes machine appliquéd using the same decorative machine stitch and thread throughout. The patches spiral into the center, overlapping the previous patches, with the final patch covering the last raw edges. If the patches were cut with bias edges, they could be appliquéd with a straight machine stitch for a ragged edge.

Stitch-and-flip crazy patchwork

Constructing crazy patchwork by machine using the stitch-and-flip method (see page 66) is quicker than appliquéing individual patches, although it is more difficult to use up irregularly shaped scraps.

Method: Follow the basic instructions for making the Log Cabin block (page 67). Begin in the center, but angle the strips as you sew them on. There is no need to cut strips to a regular length; you can use up wedge shapes and irregular strips. Antique crazy patchwork was often not quilted, but if you want to include batting, it is easy to layer it on top of the backing fabric before you begin piecing, so the patchwork and quilting are done in one step.

Ready-made Indian goldwork trims add sparkle to this silk crazy patchwork bag.

"Crazy" by Jenny Hewer
Heavily embellished crazy patchwork is good for smaller items, like this colorful modern version made into a cushion.

Techniques for textures

Simple fabric manipulation effects like tucks, points, and yo-yos add texture to your patchwork design. They can be combined with other techniques, such as crazy patchwork or appliqué. Prairie points and sawtooth triangles make interesting edge treatments too. Fabric manipulation is popular with contemporary quiltmakers but draws on traditional sources.

🔲 TRY IT

248 Prairie points strip

Make continuous prairie points from a long strip of fabric (below). It is easy to work out the length of the strip you need, because it will be the same length as the finished row of points. So, a 20 in (50.8 cm) strip of fabric will make a strip of points the same length, with the base of the points measuring 4 in (10.2 cm). The strip should be twice the width of the base of the point— 8 in (20.3 cm) in this instance. Press the strip in half along the length and cut from the edge to the center crease at 4 in (10.2 cm) intervals along one side. Cut from the edge to the center at 4 in (10.2 cm) intervals along the other long side, but make the first cut 2 in (5 cm) from the end, so the cuts are staggered.

249 Making prairie points

These triangular inserts are quickly made by folding squares of patchwork fabric. The base of the finished triangle is the same as the side of the square. A 4-in (10.2-cm) square is a manageable size—if the prairie points are too large, they won't stay neatly folded. Fold the square in half and press to make a rectangle, with wrong sides together. Fold the ends of the rectangle to meet at the center of the long raw edge and press. You have completed one prairie point.

250 Positioning prairie points

Prairie points can be inserted between patchwork seams. The right side shows the fold, so make sure this will be at the front when you have pressed the seam allowance to one side. They can also be arranged in rows along the edge of a quilt finished using the facing method (see page 132), inserted between the facing and the quilt, face down against the front of the quilt. They can be positioned to overlap one another.

251 Sawtooth triangles

By folding the square in a different way, you can make sawtooth triangles, which can be interlocked. Fold a 4 in (10.2 cm) square in half diagonally, wrong sides together, and then in half diagonally again. Press. You will have a triangle that is the same size as a prairie point made from the same basic square, but because one short side of the triangle is "open," you can arrange the sawtooth triangles to interlock.

252
Creating tucks

Essentially large pintucks, tucks can be manipulated and held down with further machine stitching to create wave effects. They are good for borders and interesting for patchwork bags.

1 | Start with a long strip of fabric—the eventual length of the strip will depend on how closely you set the pleats. If you use a striped fabric, you won't need to mark any pleat lines on your fabric and the stripe color will make a wave effect. The stripes on this fabric are ³⁄₈ in (1 cm) apart. Fold the fabric along every fourth stripe and stitch a series of ³⁄₈-in (1-cm) wide tucks. The space between each stitching line is the width of two stripes, or ³⁄₄ in (1.9 cm). If you use plain calico, you will need to mark lines at intervals four times the width of the tuck—1 in (2.5 cm) apart for ¹⁄₄ in (6 mm) tucks. Press all the tucks to one side.

2 | On the right side, stitch the tucks down, sewing along the center of the panel. Mark a guideline for this. Then press the tucks in the opposite direction on either side of the panel and stitch down to the background again, to create a wave effect. The striped fabric will make the "waves" appear to change color. Repeat the pressing and stitching to the outer edge of the panel, with the same interval between the stitched lines.

253
Using a yo-yo maker

A "quick" yo-yo maker makes the process even easier, as it is not necessary to press a hem allowance before gathering the yo-yo. The fabric is placed between the plastic plate and the disk, and trimmed around the disk. Holes in the plate allow you to space your gathering stitches evenly. Once the stitches are in place, simply remove the fabric from the plate and disk and pull up the threads. Press the finished yo-yo.

254
Making yo-yos

Also known as "Suffolk puffs," these gathered circles were popular for making lightweight bedcovers in the early twentieth century. Their use as appliquéd texture makes them appealing for modern quilters. Yo-yos are easy to make.

1 | Decide on the size of your finished yo-yo and cut a circle twice this size, say 5 in (12.5 cm) for a finished size of 2¹⁄₂ in (38 mm). Turn under a ¹⁄₄ in (6 mm) hem all around by pressing the circle around a cardboard template, ¹⁄₂ in (13 mm) smaller than the circle. Use a strong doubled thread and sew a ring of running stitch around the outer edge of the circle, stitching close to the edge, as shown. Start with a knot and leave a long tail of thread.

2 | Gather up the yo-yo by pulling gently on the ends of the thread. Pull up the gathers closely, to make the opening as small as possible. Knot the thread ends together and stitch them out of sight. Flatten out the yo-yo with the gather in the center and steam press. Make more yo-yos in the same way.

Creative use of yo-yos and beaded embellishments add textural interest (see page 99).

BATTING AND BASTING

Batting structures your quilt, and is hidden when it is finished.
Basting holds the layers temporarily in place while you quilt.

Batting

Batting is available in various different thicknesses and
different fibers. Choosing the right batting for your quilt will
make the difference between an enjoyable quilting experience
and real hard work. With the right batting, your quilt will last
longer and feel "just right."

Natural cotton
batting

Black
blended
batting

Bleached cotton
batting

FIX IT

255 *Ridges and creases*

Polyester batting is often quite
badly ridged and creased when
it is first removed from its
packaging. Heat will relax the
fibers, make the batting flatter,
and the quilt will be easier to
baste. Take the batting out of the
packaging and lay it out flat. Use
a hairdryer on a hot setting and
work your way across the quilt.
The hot air will relax and remove
those creases very quickly.

256
Choosing batting

Before you buy your quilt batting
consider several things:
• How are you going to make your quilt?
Some batting is suitable only for hand
quilting; others only for machine quilting.
• Will you want to machine wash the
quilt? Cotton and polyester will be easier
to wash than wool and silk, which
usually need to be dry-cleaned.
• Do you want a warm quilt? If you
are going to use the quilt on top of
an eiderdown or if you live in a warm
region, you may not want a thick quilt
on a bed.
• Do you want a puffy look or a flatter
finish? Polyester, wool, and silk all have
more bounce than cotton—nice for
appliqué designs and wholecloth quilts.

257
Batting sizes

Quality batting is available in various
sizes. Cut and packaged sizes include
craft—45 x 36 in (114.3 x 91.4 cm), crib—
60 x 45 in (152.4 x 114.3 cm), twin—90
x 72 in (228.6 x 182.9 cm), queen—108
x 90 in (274.3 x 228.6 cm), and king—
120 in (304.8 cm) square. It is also
available by the yard or meter, in various
widths. Select an appropriate size for
your project, allowing about 2 in (5 cm)
extra all round.

258
Weight and thickness

Batting is described by weight—2 oz
(60 g) is the thinnest, followed by
4 oz, 6 oz, and 8 oz (115 g, 180 g, and
220 g). Most quilters use a 2 oz (60 g)
batting. Thicker battings are progressively
harder to quilt through nicely and large
pieces are bulky to handle for machine
quilting. "Request weight" cotton is even
thinner than 2 oz (60 g) batting.

Weight does not necessarily reflect
the apparent thickness of batting, as
6 oz (180 g) compressed polyester
batting does not look particularly thick
but is, as you would expect, quite stiff
and dense. You may also see references
to "loft," which refer to the thickness of
the batting—think of it as the amount
of "bounce" batting has.

Prizewinning hand quilters almost
always use thin batting, which enables
them to quilt more stitches to the inch
and use smaller stitches. Polyester
"request weight" batting is even easier
to quilt than thin cotton batting.

259 Fiber content

Natural fibers include cotton, wool, silk, alpaca, and most recently, bamboo fiber. Manmade quilt battings are made from polyester. There are also cotton and polyester blends; usually 80 percent cotton to 20 percent polyester. Wool and polyester blends are made in a similar ratio.

Natural fibers breathe well but are not as easy to wash as polyester. Cotton batting is heavy when wet and a large quilt may upset the sensors on your washing machine.

260 Batting colors

Cotton batting is available in natural (cream) and bleached (white). Cotton/polyester is also available in black, which is good for very dark-colored quilts. Polyester is available in black or white. Wool, silk, alpaca, and bamboo are unbleached. Some cotton batting is organic—information about this will be on the label. Some natural cotton battings may have seed heads in them, which could shadow through the top of a light-colored quilt and make it appear gritty, so choose carefully.

261 Shrinkage

Most cotton and cotton-blend battings are designed to shrink when washed for the first time, from one to five percent. If you use one of these battings and quilt it quite closely, you can get the instant antique look when you wash it for the first time, as the batting will pucker up, making it look like an old quilt. If you do not want this look, presoak the batting in the bath or shower for around 15 minutes, first with very hot water then with cold, to "shock" the fibers into shrinking. Squeeze out as much water as possible, spin the batting in the washing machine and, if possible, tumble-dry it on a low heat-setting to fluff up the fibers. This will remove any resins used in manufacture and the batting will be bouncy and easy to quilt.

262 Machine and hand batting

Some batting is only suitable for hand quilting, and others are only suitable for machine. A good batting for hand quilting is designed to allow the needle to pass through easily and may be too slippery for machine quilting—where you want the batting to cling to the quilt slightly—causing the quilt to pucker under the needle.

Some machine battings have a cotton scrim embedded in them, which means you can quilt larger distances apart. However, the scrim makes hand quilting hard work, as it resists the quilting needle. Many battings are suitable for either hand or machine quilting, so choose one of these if you intend to combine both techniques in one project.

263 Cheap batting

You may have heard horror stories about cheap, unbranded batting breaking down inside a quilt or "bearding," where individual fibers work their way through the quilt top. Unfortunately there is no remedy for this—bearding will only get worse if you try to remove the fibers—so remember that cheap batting is usually a false economy.

The price difference between a good quality, branded batting from a reputable quilt store and cheap batting is really quite small, so make the extra little bit of investment in a good batting. You may be spending the same amount of time quilting as you did preparing the quilt top, so you don't want to be fighting poor quality batting all the way!

Blended batting adds loft without the weight of pure cotton.

FIX IT

264 How close can I quilt?

Different battings have different minimum quilting distances, governing how far apart you have to quilt to prevent the batting breaking up and migrating inside the quilt when in use. This can be as little as 3 in (7.5 cm) or as much as 10 in (25 cm) apart, depending on the type of batting fiber, whether it is needlepunched (a mechanical production process which partially felts the batting), or if it has a scrim inside. For a wallhanging, you can push the distance to the limit, although over a long period the batting may tend to migrate to the bottom of the quilt. For bed quilts and throws, stick to the recommended minimum distance. Stitching close together, say a $3/8$ in (1 cm) grid, is better suited to wallhangings, cushions, and bags, as very close quilting tends to make a quilt stiff and unable to drape well.

Making the quilt sandwich

There are several ways you can baste your quilt, batting, and backing fabric together—commonly known as "making the quilt sandwich." The layers need to be held together securely so you can quilt, either by pinning or stitching. If you want to quilt an elaborate design, you may want to mark the top for quilting before making the sandwich (see page 109), but simple quilting designs can be marked afterwards.

The back of "Japanese Fans" (page 75), pieced in three strips.

265 Choosing backing fabric

You will need to prepare a backing for your quilt that is slightly larger than the quilt top; about 2 in (5 cm) larger all around. While it is possible to purchase fabrics 108 in (274.3 cm) wide, many quilters piece the backing fabric from two or more widths of quilting cotton. You may not want to put expensive fabric on the back of your quilt, where it won't be seen very much, but the backing fabric does need to relate to the quilt top in some way (usually they are color-coordinated). Check that patterned backing doesn't shadow through the batting and quilt top.

The back of the quilt should be a similar quality and weight to the front. Polycotton or cotton sheeting does not make a good quilt backing, as the thread count is high and the fabric tightly woven, so it is hard to quilt, especially by hand. Look out for sales at quilting stores where past-season fabric bargains are included—if you have been making your quilt top over a few months, you may even find one of the fabrics in clearance by the time you come to quilt it.

266 Using the backing fabric

Wash and press the backing fabric before use. Join pieces to make the backing so the seams don't fall where the quilt may be repeatedly folded; it is better to have a seam down either side of the backing than straight down the center, for example. Make a ³/₈ in (1 cm) seam allowance and press the seams open to reduce bulk. If you don't have enough of one fabric, try creating a simple strip-pieced design as shown here; or use your preferred backing fabric to border a center section made from something else, so the "best" backing fabric will be visible when the quilt is turned back. Creating another, simpler patchwork design on the back of a quilt has become popular. It can be a useful way to extend the length of a quilt backing, as shown here. Keep the patchwork simple if you don't want to have to quilt through lots of seams in the backing as well as the top of the quilt.

267 The importance of layering

Whichever method you use to hold the layers of the quilt sandwich together, you will make the sandwich with the backing fabric wrong side up, the batting on top of the backing and the quilt top on top of that, right side up. If you choose to bag out your quilt rather than binding it, you will need to layer the quilt, backing, and batting in a different order (see page 104). If you want to add extra three-dimensional effects using trapunto or corded quilting (page 122), this will need to be worked before basting the whole quilt together. The backing needs to be secured tightly while the layers are pinned or basted together.

268 Pinning or stitching?

Some quilters prefer to pin or baste the layers; others prefer to stitch. Special curved safety pins are available, which are easier to insert than ordinary pins. Check that any pins you plan to use won't rust in your quilt—they may be there for some time if you are hand quilting. Take care only to pin through patterned fabrics, as the pins can leave tiny holes. Pins can be removed easily as quilting progresses.

Stitching with long basting stitches doesn't take much longer than basting with pins. Use a large sharp or longer crewel needle and proper cotton basting thread, which is soft, breaks readily, and will be easier to remove than a mixture of leftover threads. Threading a pincushion full of needles at the start speeds up your work; or alternately, ask some friends to help you baste. Basting at 2 in (5 cm) intervals holds the layers very securely for hand quilting and is essential if you want to quilt without a frame or hoop. Try basting with diagonal stitches, as shown below, or baste in a grid.

TRY IT

270 Use a teaspoon

Use a teaspoon to lever up the point of the needle after each stitch to prevent your fingers getting sore. Although it may feel awkward at first, you will be able to baste much more quickly and efficiently with a spoon, so persevere until you can do it. The edge of the spoon eventually becomes nicked by the needle, so use an old spoon—not your best.

TRY IT

269 Basting on a table

Basting the layers on a table is easy to do and reduces backache. The table does not need to be as large as the quilt—you can baste a section and pull the quilt over the table to continue basting.

• Smooth out the backing on a flat, clean surface, covering an important tabletop with heavy card or wooden sheeting. Hold the edges down with masking tape at intervals. Spread the batting on top and smooth out. Deal with a large piece of batting by folding it into quarters, lining up one corner with the backing corner and opening it out. The top can be folded, lined up, and unfolded the same way.

• Lay the quilt top over the batting and smooth it out, making sure block corners are square—check that corners are square and straight lines are straight with your quilting rulers. Start at the center and baste the layers together. You can stitch lines radiating from the center or follow the grid method.

• For hand quilting, trim off the batting to ½ in (13 mm) larger than the quilt top and the backing to approximately 2 in (5 cm) larger; wrap the backing over the batting and quilt edge, folding the backing edge under; and baste. This will keep batting fibers from creeping out of the edges as you quilt. For machine quilting, trim the batting and backing to ½ in (13 mm) larger than the quilt top all around.

271 Basting on a frame

A traditional quilt frame can be useful for basting, even if you do not intend to actually quilt on the frame. A frame normally consists of two rollers (with battens or dowels at the front and back) and two sidepieces, which pass through slots cut in the ends of the rollers. (See page 111 for how to construct a frame.) The quilt can be quilted on the frame without any further basting, or it can be basted on the frame, removed, and then quilted in a hoop or lap-quilted without any frame.

QUILTING DESIGNS AND TECHNIQUES

Quilting does the job of holding the quilt top, batting, and backing together. It can be as simple or as elaborate as you wish.

The quilting pattern

Good quilting can make all the difference between an average and a really beautiful quilt, so consider various quilting options before you begin. The quilting pattern should enhance your quilt design rather than conflict with it.

272 Choosing a pattern

Not every quilt requires an elaborate quilting pattern. Printed fabrics can camouflage the quilting, so ornate traditional wreaths and feathers are almost invisible. Simpler quilting requires minimal or no marking and may be more suited to your quilt, especially if there is already a lot of pattern in the quilt top.

273 Echo quilting

Often used for Hawaiian designs it a good way to quilt the background of appliqué motifs. Hawaiian quilters quilt rows a finger-width apart. Mark the consecutive lines on the background fabric as a quilting guide if you prefer.

Echo quilting emphasizes appliqué motifs.

274 In the ditch

The stitches follow the patchwork seam lines or the appliqué outlines. Whether quilted by hand or machine, the stitches sit on the side of the seam away from where the seam allowance has been pressed. This method is easy to hand quilt, but machine quilting takes practice to stay in the ditch and not wobble out of it. Use a walking foot.

Hand quilting in the ditch.

275 Contour quilting

Quilting a consistent $\frac{1}{4}$ in (6 mm) or $\frac{3}{8}$ in (1 cm) away from seam lines emphasizes the patchwork shapes. Mark guidelines for hand quilting, which can be drawn on the quilt top or with $\frac{1}{4}$ in (6 mm) masking tape. For machine quilting, use the width of the walking foot to stitch $\frac{3}{8}$ in (1 cm) away from the seam lines.

276 Cross hatching

A simple grid of lines—either square or at an angle—makes a good contrast with curved quilting patterns, or use it for a utilitarian quilting style. Lines can be drawn on the quilt top with a ruler or marked with 1 in (2.5 cm) wide masking tape. To machine quilt, use the quilting bar to space consecutive lines, making sure the end of the bar is running along the previous row of stitches each time.

Hatching can make a striking impact.

277 Marking quilting patterns

Pencils, pen, and masking tape are all useful for marking quilt designs onto the quilt top. Simple quilting designs require minimal marking. Elaborate, traditional designs may require templates and patterns. There are plenty of specialist sources for these, whether ready-made templates and stencils or pattern books. Designs include medallion motifs for large patches (below right), border patterns used at the edges of quilts or as frames (below left), and background designs used to fill in around patterns.

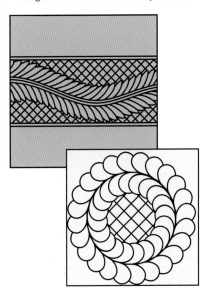

278 Using templates

English North-Country quilts were traditionally marked using templates. Quilters marked around the templates and filled in the details, such as the inside of feathers, by hand. Many old quilts still have the pencil marks intact and were marked with a blue crayon. These designs are similar to those seen on Amish quilts, particularly medallion designs. Make your own collection of templates by tracing or photocopying the pattern you want to use and gluing it to a piece of recycled cardboard. For a more modern approach, use a piece of template plastic or recycle some plastic packaging to make your templates. Other quilting designs were marked by drawing around household objects, such as cups and dishes. Baptist Fans, a traditional design (below), could be marked using a dinner plate for the outer curve, with consecutive curves a finger-width away.

FIX IT

279 *Not enough quilting?*

Many potentially beautiful quilts are spoiled by "not enough quilting." Some parts of the quilt top may have more quilting than others and, frequently, the background is ignored, so that it puffs up just as much as the quilted designs and detracts from them. A cross-hatched grid is an easy fix for this problem, as it complements and emphasizes the curves in the main quilting design while also flattening the background.

This small wholecloth quilt captures the essence of the English North Country quilt tradition with typical design features—a border and center combining several related motifs linked with cross hatching. "North Country Quilt" by Lilian Hedley, Size 24 in (61 cm) square.

TRY IT

280 Audition your design

If you are not sure how a quilting pattern will look on your quilt top, use quilting lines drawn on a piece of transparent plastic to "audition" a design. Many items are packaged in clear plastic, so it is easy to recycle pieces big enough for quilt designs. Trace the design onto the plastic using a permanent marker, dashing the lines to look like stitching. Lay the plastic over the quilt top and see if you like how it looks.

281 Tracing a design

Unless you are marking a very elaborate quilting design from a pattern that needs tracing onto the quilt using a lightbox, it is more reliable to mark your quilting design after basting the quilt sandwich, as your marking lines might become smudged or faded during the basting process. To transfer a large design to a quilt top, improvise a lightbox by taping the pattern to a large window or patio door, taping the fabric over it and tracing through. You will need strong daylight to do this, and a light in the room behind you may be necessary so you can see the lines you are drawing.

Hand quilting

Hand quilting can be done with the quilt in a hoop, on a frame, or in your lap. Issues such as portability will affect your choice of method—lap quilting can be taken almost anywhere while a frame will restrict you to quilting in one room.

283 Where to start?

Many quilters believe that you must begin quilting from the center, easing out excess fullness in the quilt and batting as you go, preventing unsightly rucks. It also deals with excess fullness around the quilt border, if the quilt has been allowed to "grow" around the edges as subsequent borders are added (see page 139). But if you have followed the instructions earlier in this book (see pages 80–81), your quilt top will be flat and well basted, so these issues won't be a problem.

In theory, you can start quilting anywhere. Deal with the larger design elements first and work down to the smaller ones. If your quilt has sashing, quilt either side of the sashing, in the ditch, and deal with each block individually.

TRY IT

282 Two-thimble quilting

To be able to quilt with even stitches and for a long time, wear two thimbles to quilt; one on the middle finger of each hand. The thimble on your right hand needs to hold the back of the needle, so look for a thimble with a dimple in the middle or a ridge around it. The thimble on your left hand needs a rounded edge, so you can flick the point of the needle off the edge of the thimble, pushing it back up through the quilt (you may hear the needle "click" as it comes off the thimble edge). There are different kinds of thimbles available, including traditional metal thimbles, leather thimbles, and plastic thimbles, so try out several until you find the ones you like best.

284 Basic technique

From the front of the quilt, make a long stitch in the opposite direction to the way you will quilt, along the stitching line, and "pop" the two knots through the fabric and into the batting. Insert the needle perpendicular to the quilt each time. With your left hand under the quilt, take several small running stitches at a time, going through all the layers, before pulling the thread through. At the end, turn the quilt over, tie two more knots, and pop these through the backing and into the quilt.

285 Easy hand quilting

The hand quilting stitch is basically running stitch, but each stitch must go through all the layers and be as even as possible. It is more important that the stitches be even rather than tiny. To hand quilt, thread the needle with an 18 in (45.7 cm) length of thread and make two knots about ½ in (1.3 cm) apart, by making a loop and passing the end of the thread through it several times.

286 Choosing needles

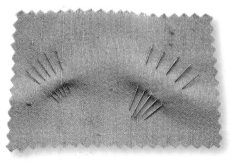

Most quilters use "betweens"— short quilting needles that sit comfortably in the tip of a thimble. Use a between to quilt with two thimbles. Use a larger between, such as a no. 10, when you first quilt this way, and a smaller one, such as a no. 12, as you become more adept. If you are not using the twin thimble method, try a no. 9 or no. 10 sharp, which are longer and easier to hold.

287 Choosing threads

Use a hand quilting thread if possible, ready waxed so it will pass through the quilt easily. If you cannot get the color you want, use a 50s sewing cotton and wax the thread. A shaded thread may blend in better than a plain one if you are quilting printed fabrics. Thicker, contrasting threads and larger stitches are used for "big stitch" quilting (see page 124), with larger needles or embroidery "crewels" for the heavier threads.

288 Quilting in a hoop

Using a quilting hoop will help you maintain an even tension when hand quilting. Quilting hoops are deeper and larger than embroidery hoops, such as 16 in (40.6 cm) or 18 in (45.7 cm) in diameter. It should be large enough to prop up in your left arm (right arm for left-handed quilters) or against the edge of a table, with hands free to work.

Turn the hoop to follow the direction of your stitching. Hoops with floor stands fully support your work. To prepare the frame, wrap bias tape around the center hoop, so it grips your quilt. Drape the quilt over the center, on the section you want to quilt first, place the outer hoop over it, and tighten up the clamp. The quilt should be fairly taut, but not tight or distorted. Baste or pin a strip of scrap fabric along the quilt edge, so you have something to fasten into the hoop. Hoops are portable and easily carried from room to room or to your quilt group.

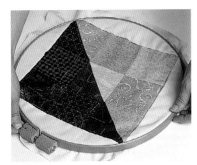

289 Quilting frames

Taking up more space than hoops, frames need to be longer than the shortest side of your quilt. Some modern frames require no basting, and some can be folded flat to the wall when not in use. Traditional frames are made from four pieces of wood—two rollers (which may be flat laths) and two end pieces—supported at each end, on trestles or the backs of dining chairs.

Getting the height comfortable for working can be tricky. They can lean flat against a wall when you are not quilting and be taken apart completely when not in use. Either frame holds the quilt under an even tension. You will need to learn to stitch in all directions, quilting progressively across the design. Keeping more than one needle and thread in play is more efficient, as you can work your way along the quilt, stitching different parts of the quilt design simultaneously.

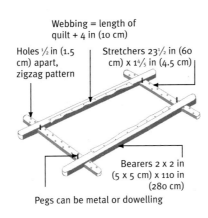

Webbing = length of quilt + 4 in (10 cm)

Holes ½ in (1.5 cm) apart, zigzag pattern

Stretchers 23½ in (60 cm) x 1⁴⁄₅ in (4.5 cm)

Bearers 2 x 2 in (5 x 5 cm) x 110 in (280 cm)

Pegs can be metal or dowelling

291 Lap quilting

A hoop or frame is not required for this quilting method, but your quilt sandwich needs to be basted closely, with stitch lines about 2 in (5 cm) apart. Basting with pins is not really adequate. Drape the quilt across your body and allow it to partly lie on the floor (make sure the floor is clean, or spread out a sheet under your work). You will be using gravity to help you maintain tension on the quilt. Work with your left arm under the quilt, supporting it. The twin thimble technique does not work for lap quilting, so use a sharp rather than a between as your quilting needle. Because the quilt is across your lap, it is great for quilting in cold climates but too warm if you are quilting in hot weather.

FIX IT

290 *Quilt gone baggy or become a bed for the cat?*

Remember to remove your work from the hoop when you are not quilting. Leaving it on the hoop for long periods can make the quilt stretch and go baggy. Quilts in hoops (and on flat frames) are attractive sleeping places for cats, and you really don't want to find your work covered in hairs and stretched out of shape. Takenoko the cat loves his old quilt and it keeps him off work in progress.

Machine quilting

Machine quilting produces a more distinct line than the softer line of hand quilting, and is highly regarded as a technique in its own right, not simply as a substitute for hand quilting. It can be sewn in two ways—with a walking foot or in free-motion, using a darning or embroidery foot.

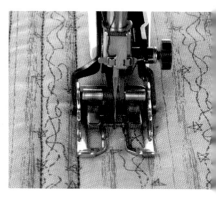

292

Tips for perfect machine quilting

• Start and finish machine quilting at the edge of the quilt whenever you can, to avoid lots of loose thread ends to sew in afterward.

• Continuous line patterns are easiest to quilt. If you are adapting a hand-quilting pattern, minimize stopping and starting by "reversing" over parts of the pattern if necessary.

• Many modern machines have a "needle down" button, so the needle is in the fabric whenever you stop—select this option for machine quilting, so the needle holds your work in place when you raise the walking foot to turn a corner or pause during free-motion quilting (the darning foot will release the fabric when the needle is "up").

• Use a "quilting" machine needle, which is designed to stitch through the thickness of batting and fabrics, to improve stitch quality; and a "metallica" needle if you are using metallic thread. Other needles may skip stitches through thicker batting.

• You may need to rethread the bobbin to achieve a tighter bobbin tension—check your machine manual for advice—particularly for free-motion quilting. Stitch a small test sample if you are not sure.

• Use the same weight thread in the bobbin as on top, matching the color to the backing fabric. If the tension is set correctly, the bobbin thread will be buried in the thickness of the quilt and you won't see it on top of the stitch.

• Use a straight stitch plate on the machine, if you have one, for all straight stitching. It will prevent the needle from accidentally being dragged sideways as you quilt, particularly when free-motion quilting.

• Manage the bulk of the quilt under the machine arm (the "harp") by rolling or loosely bunching it up.

• The quilt must be supported adequately behind and to the side of the machine, or you will be fighting gravity! A larger machine extension table helps—these are available for all machines.

• Remember to take frequent breaks. Machine quilting is quite physically tiring and it is essential that your machine is at a comfortable height for sewing.

• Choose toning thread a shade darker than the background fabric, unless you want a contrast. The samples shown here use red thread for clarity, showing quilting with the walking foot (above) and free-motion quilting (opposite below right).

• Clean your machine to stop lint from the batting building up around the bobbin, which could cause stitching problems.

293

How to start?

If you can start and finish stitching at the edge of the quilt, there is no need to finish off threads but, depending on your quilting design, this is not always possible. If you are machine quilting a traditional hand-quilt design, you are likely to have quite a few stops and starts. Newer machines can stitch on the spot to finish off the thread ends or you can sew the last few stitches with a very short stitch length. Some quilters like to sew a couple of stitches in reverse at the start and finish of each quilting line.

For a high-quality finish, begin by making two stitches. With the needle holding your work in the "down" position, pull the bobbin thread through to the top of your quilt, by pulling gently on the top thread. With both threads on top, you can continue without risking catching the bobbin tail in subsequent stitches.

294

Finishing techniques

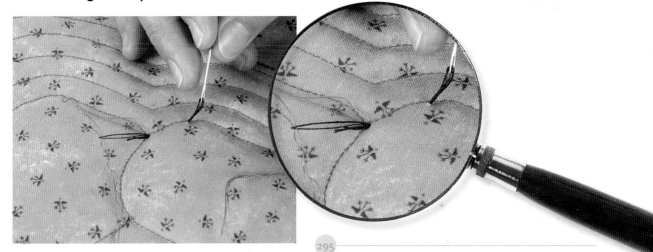

When you finish quilting, knot the thread ends together and thread them back into the quilt. Thread a needle with a short length of doubled thread. Use this thread loop to lasso the thread ends and pull them into the quilt, saving time on repeatedly threading your needle with all the ends.

There is no need to have all the waste thread embedded in the quilt batting. When you finish quilting, knot the thread ends together and thread them back into the quilt. Even the shortest thread tail can be finished off this way.

Wavy lines
quilted with the
walking foot and
a utility stitch.

296

Machine quilting with the walking foot

A walking foot feeds the quilt top and backing through at the same rate, preventing unsightly puckering, by synchronizing the feed dogs and the needle. The foot is linked to the needle motion via a screw that holds the needle in the needle bar. A walking foot is good for quilting straight lines, "in the ditch" (in the seam line), parallel lines, grids, and gentle curves. Sharp changes in direction will require turning the quilt while it is on the machine—this is physically very difficult with a large piece of quilting. With the zigzag throat plate, use the walking foot to quilt fancy embroidery stitches on computerized machines. Some utility stitches are also good for quilting.

295

Free-motion quilting

Free-motion quilting is done with the machine feed dogs set down (you need to cover the feed dogs with a small plate on some older machines) and a darning, quilting, or embroidery foot. This foot has a built-in spring, so it moves up and down on the fabric with the needle action. Without the feed dogs engaged, you are free to move the quilt through the machine in any direction, including side to side.

The quilt must be moved evenly to maintain a consistent stitch length and you need to run the machine at a constant speed. Some computerized machines have a movement sensor that regulates the stitching speed for even stitches. Stippling is a popular way of filling in backgrounds—a bit like doodling on fabric. If the thread breaks, try changing the needle and check the tension. You may need to slow down your stitching speed.

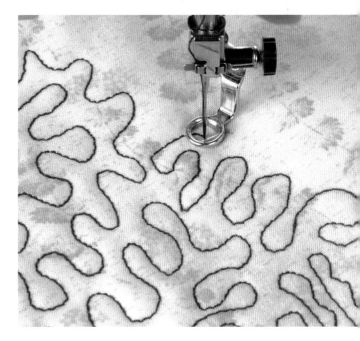

Free-motion quilting in
a meander pattern with
the embroidery foot.

Long-arm machine quilting

Long-arm machine quilting services have become popular over the last few years. Most quilters don't have space for the large quilting frame at home, but you can send your quilt top to be "long-armed" by a professional quilter if you don't want to quilt it yourself. It's a good way to deal with a backlog of quilt tops.

297 How the long-arm machine works

This kind of machine quilting is stitched on a long-arm straight stitch machine mounted on a metal quilt frame. Machine and frame represent a much larger investment than a domestic machine. As its name suggests, the machine is much longer than a domestic sewing machine, with a larger "harp" or working area under the arm. To stitch, the machine moves instead of the quilt. A light, responsive tracking system enables the quilter to guide the machine across the quilt surface in any direction, standing facing the machine head instead of sitting in front of the machine. Because the machine can stitch easily in any direction, long-arm quilting patterns often favor large-scale sweeping curves; the kind of design that would be difficult to quilt on a domestic machine. Modern long-arm machines have features such as stitch regulators for consistent stitch length and can be fully computer-guided if necessary.

FIX IT

298 *Backing too small to quilt?*

If your backing fabric is only an inch or two larger than the quilt, there won't be enough backing to attach the quilt to the frame while keeping enough of the quilt accessible all around for the machine to stitch the quilting right up to the edge. You may be able to solve the problem by sewing a 2–3 in (5–7.6 cm) strip to each edge of the backing. Check with the quilter that they will be able to work with this.

299 What to provide

You need to provide the quilt backing as well as the quilt top. The backing fabric usually needs to be 3 in (7.5 cm) larger all around than the quilt—but check this with your quilter. Threads are usually supplied by the quilter, as not all threads will quilt well on a long-arm machine running at high speeds. Shaded threads are a good choice for pantograph or simple designs where the same thread will be used over the whole quilt. The quilter can usually supply batting, too.

300
When the quilting's done

The quilt will be returned to you for trimming and binding, unless the quilter offers a binding service. If the quilter has trimmed the edge for you, the scrap backing strips will be returned with your quilt. Some long-arm quilters offer a basting service, so you can still hand quilt your project if you wish even if you don't have the time and space to baste it yourself.

Some competitive quilt shows have categories for long-arm quilted work or may allow long-arm quilts in a two-person category (see page 146). If you enter a quilt that has been professionally quilted into a show, you must make sure you are entering it in the right category and give the quilter's name as well as your own. It would be courteous to let them know that you are entering the quilt, rather than surprising them if they visit the show. If a prize is awarded that relates solely to the quilting, it should go to the quilter.

"Guide Me" by Ferret
A design inspired by traditional wholecloth and pieced quilts. Free-motion long-arm quilting like this needs considerable skill. Like most wholecloths, it is reversible. The detail, below, shows how the colored threads create the design from different quilting patterns. Size 96 in (244 cm) square.

"Perttu" by Ferret
Long-arm quilting breaks traditional design boundaries for pictorial work in this appliquéd and free-motion long-arm quilted portrait of cellist Perttu Kivilakso of Apocalyptica. Size 30 x 16 in (76 x 41 cm).

301
Custom quilting

Custom, or bespoke, quilting, designed specially for your quilt, takes much longer and is at the "heirloom" end of long-arm quilting services. You will need to discuss in detail the kind of quilting you want, selecting the patterns and threads. Let the professional quilter help you choose— they will have a lot of experience of this kind of quilting and will be able to advise you as to what is best for your quilt.

302
Using a long-arm quilting service

The best long-arm quilting services are usually very busy and it is a good idea to find out in advance if the quilter has a waiting list. Don't expect them to be able to quilt your work next week! Many long-arm quilters offer a basic pantograph quilting service, where the machine is guided along an edge-to-edge continuous pattern sheet and stitched in one thread. Typical patterns have large scrolling designs and the pattern will repeat across the quilt.

Other quilters offer simple hand-guided patterns as their basic service. You may be offered the option of a different design in the borders or additional thread colors. The denser and more elaborate the quilting, the higher the fee will be.

TRY IT

303 Pantograph designs

All-over pantograph designs are a good choice for utility quilts, such as a quilt you might give a student to take away to college. You will be able to choose from a range of designs. The quilter may suggest one that echoes your patchwork pattern or a fabric motif. Shaded threads are very effective for these simpler repeat designs. Pantograph or simple long-arm quilting is also a good choice for a fundraising quilt made by a quilt group (see group projects, page 138).

Quilt-as-you-go

If you want to machine quilt but dread dealing with a large quilt in one piece, then "quilt-as-you-go" (QAYG) is the technique for you. The work is quilted in manageable sections no larger than a cushion cover or small panel, so it is easy to handle.

304

QAYG with sashing strips

In this method, batting is sandwiched between each completed part of the quilt and the backing blocks—and quilted individually, before being stitched to the next section. You never need to maneuver a large piece of quilting on the machine. Small pieces can be turned easily, so you can quilt unobtrusively in the ditch along the seam lines in spirals or zigzags—difficult to do with a full-size quilt. The disadvantage is the amount of hand finishing required, as each sashing strip on the back has to be hemmed down by hand.

You should use the same kind of batting throughout. The sashing strips are 1 in (2.5 cm) wide, so the finished sashing is just ½ in (1.3 cm). This width works with the ¼ in (6 mm) seam allowance, so the batting in one block butts up right against the next, and there is no need to add extra batting.

1 | Cut the backing and batting squares slightly larger than your quilt block and pin together with the block to make a quilt sandwich (see page 66), checking that the block is square. Machine quilt as desired. Use your rotary cutter and ruler to trim the finished blocks to the same size. If you are designing a project with differently sized blocks, remember to allow for the ½ in (13 mm) sashing.

2| Pin a sashing strip to one side of the block, right sides together. Pin a second sashing strip to the back of the block. Machine sew both sashing strips to the block, with a ¼ in (6 mm) seam allowance.

3 | With the block facing upward, flip over the sashing strip on the right side of the block and finger-press it, by running your finger firmly along the seam with the block on a firm surface. With right sides together, pin the sashing strip sewn to the front of the block to the next quilted block, and sew together with a ¼-in (6-mm) seam allowance. Finger-press the seam.

4| Turn the work over and finger-press the sashing strip on the back. Keeping the work as flat as possible, turn under the raw edge of the sashing strip to align with where the front sashing strip is stitched to the block. Pin and stitch in place, with the same hemstitch used to finish off the quilt binding (see page 126). You do not need to stitch the batting together at the joins, as the sashing will hold it together adequately.

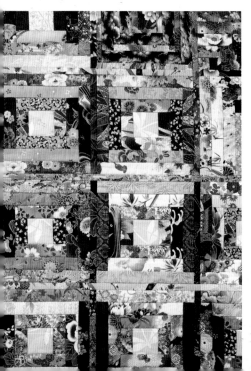

Using assorted fabrics for the sashing makes it blend with the Log Cabin strips. See Oriental Log Cabin sampler, page 37.

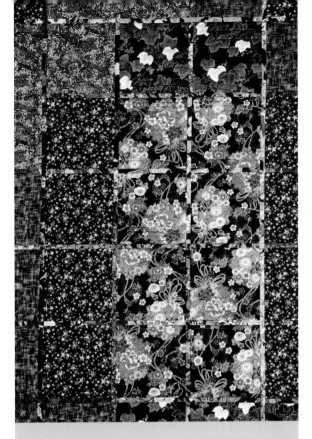

FIX IT

305 Sashing problems?

The sashing strips increase in length as you assemble the quilt, so you will have had plenty of practice doing the hand sewing by the time you reach the longer strips. Putting the quilt together is easier if you:

• Plan the quilt according to the sashing you have available. If you have lots of shorter pieces only the width of the block, piece the quilt in strips, then piece the strips together.

• Assemble the back in sections. Sew pairs of blocks together, then groups of four, then strips of eight.

• Check that you are sewing the blocks together in the right order as you pin the sashing strips. Take a reference photo of the quilt blocks laid out as you want them and check against this.

• Measure and cut the longer sashing strips as you go, rather than trying to work out complicated math! You will probably need to join strips for the longest sashing sections, so press seams open to reduce bulk.

• Sew the blocks together to make the quilt in two halves, joining them at the end.

TRY IT

306 Different backing fabrics

Using different backing fabrics for different parts of the quilt gives the option of a reversible design (above). Depending on the variety of blocks in your quilt, you may want to plan the position of various fabrics on the quilt back. Or, as shown here, backing different sets of blocks in a sampler quilt with the same fabric will produce a design that echoes the front of the quilt (see "Oriental Log Cabin" sampler quilt, page 37).

"Celtic Fantasy" by Diane Abram
Quilt-as-you-go sashing strips can be fully integrated into your quilt design, as used here to make narrow outlines to the bias tape appliqué blocks. Working with smaller pieces made the detailed quilting easier to achieve to a high standard. Size 85 x 61 in (216 x 155 cm).

Sashiko and kantha

Sashiko and kantha are traditional stitching techniques from Japan and Bangladesh respectively, and have become a popular part of the quilting repertoire. They are both perfect techniques for decorative quilting that is meant to be seen.

FIX IT

307 *Finding stitching hard work?*

The right fabric, thread, and needles make stitching easier. Sashiko fabric needs to have a lower thread count than normal patchwork fabrics, or it will be hard to stitch. Fabrics woven specially for sashiko are available in many colors and imitate antique cotton fabric. Special sashiko threads are available and make stitching with the doubled thread easier. Kantha needs cotton with a loose weave and may be stitched with embroidery threads, such as perlé, coton à broder, or stranded cotton. Select a sashiko needle, a large sharp, or a crewel (embroidery) needle—it must be sharp, rigid, and long, with a large eye for the thicker threads.

308

Marking pictorial designs

For darker sashiko fabrics, use a lightbox, with the pattern under the fabric, or chaco paper (Japanese dressmaker's carbon paper) to transfer more elaborate designs. Chaco paper is available in white, yellow, pink, and blue, and the marks from it wash out. Traditional Japanese family crests, or kamon, make good designs—enlarge them with a photocopier.

1| Put the chaco paper face down on the fabric with the pattern on top and pin them together. Trace along all the design lines with a ballpoint transfer tool, the end of a knitting needle, or something similar.

2| The pattern will transfer onto the cloth. Chaco paper can be reused again and again. Light-colored fabrics for kantha may be marked by placing a pattern under the fabric and tracing the design with a quilting pencil.

309

Sashiko basics

Sashiko was traditionally stitched on hemp and cotton work clothes and household textiles to make them warmer, stronger, and more hardwearing. Everyday sashiko was plain, but sashiko for special occasions featured elaborate designs, all worked in running stitch (right). Traditional Japanese patterns were used, copied from other design sources. Kamon crests were often stitched onto furoshiki wrapping cloths, to identify the owner. Old sashiko uses mostly blue and white combinations, but nowadays sashiko is stitched with other colors. Traditionally, sashiko is not stitched through batting but may be backed with a piece of old fabric—try muslin for a similar effect—or stitch sashiko as embroidery, adding extra quilting to the finished quilt. A doubled thread makes the stitches bold.

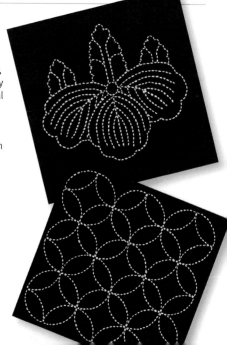

310 Stitching action

For both techniques, pleat the fabric onto the tip of the needle, making as many stitches as possible, before pulling the needle through and smoothing the stitches out.

For sashiko, this stitching action will make the two strands of thread lie parallel in the stitch, so the stitches look bold. Keep sewing straight and evenly by making as many stitches as possible with the needle before pulling the thread through. Stitches should be even and between $\frac{1}{8}$ in and $\frac{1}{4}$ in (3 and 6 mm) long. The gaps between them are about half the length of the stitch. If your stitches are not even enough, snip off the starting knot, pull out your stitches and start again. You are aiming for nice fat running stitches where the two threads lie parallel, and are slightly raised on the fabric surface. Keep the sashiko thread continuous as much as possible.

312 Kantha basics

Recycled cotton saris were the popular fabric for kantha, which is also sewn with running stitch. Colored threads are used to sew an outline, which is then filled in with consecutive stitch lines in various colors, while the background is stitched with matching thread. Stylized pictorial and geometric designs may be combined. Like sashiko, kantha is traditionally sewn through multiple fabric layers, without batting. If you want to try either technique with batting, use the thinnest available (see page 105).

Rows of running stitches are worked from the outline inward, filling in the motif.

314 Marking geometric sashiko designs

1 | Draw directly onto the fabric with a fabric marker—white marking pens, tailor's chalk, soft white watercolor pencils, quilting pencils, Japanese chaco liners, or other light colored markers are all suitable. Use the grid on a cutting mat to mark the base grid. Make sure you can see the mat's grid all around the edge. The ruler should be long enough to reach opposite sides of the mat.

2 | Mark curved lines for patterns like *Shippo* (Seven Treasures, opposite). Select a circle template with the same radius measurement as the grid. If you cut your own circle template, you can make the grid any size you like, so the design fits your project pieces.

311 Threading the needle

For sashiko, thread your needle with a whole length of thread and double it. Smooth the thread down, so it doesn't twist around itself, and tie a single knot at the end. This way the thread can't fall out of your needle if you drop it. A double thread is traditional in sashiko; use a single thread for kantha.

Start and finish stitching with a knot on the back for sashiko and "pop the knot" for kantha (see left). Follow the stitching sequence given for geometric sashiko patterns. For kamon crests, keep the thread continuous as much as possible, outlining motifs first before filling them in. Kantha motifs should be outlined first, then filled in with consecutive rows of stitching, changing thread colors to emphasize different parts of the motif.

313 Stitching sequence

Geometric sashiko patterns have traditional stitching sequences, to help you work your way around the pattern with as few stops and starts as possible. Follow the stitching directions, as shown by the arrows on the traditional Shippo (Seven Treasures) design, below. If you don't have instructions for a stitching sequence, try working it out by tracing a route around a pattern without taking your finger off the pattern line.

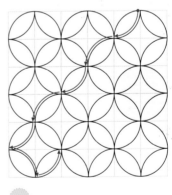

315 Finishing off

When you have stitched the whole of the motif outline, tie a single knot at the back and trim the thread. For kantha, pop the knot as you would for hand quilting. Press lightly from the back.

Hand quilting with other stitches

Many embroidery stitches can be used successfully for quilting and add an interesting texture, whether to simple patchwork, appliqué, or wholecloth quilting designs. Experiment with different stitches and try out those you feel are most effective for your project.

▓ TRY IT

316 Stitch sampler

A stitch sampler, with a simple design on plain fabric, is a good way to experiment with different stitch patterns, as the plain background won't detract from the stitches. Try out different stitches and different threads on the same piece.

"Flower Scroll Cushion" by Jenny Hewer
Various embroidery stitches were used to quilt this cushion, including chain stitch for the scrolls and flower petals. A calico panel, colored using transfer crayons applied through a freezer paper stencil, provided the inspiration to finish the design with floral motifs. Size 18 in (46 cm) square.

317 Suitable stitches

Not all embroidery stitches will work well as quilting stitches. Those that can hold the quilt layers together and are neat on the back are good for quilts. Stitches that are worked in a frame and must be held under tension, like tent stitch, would not be a good choice. The more elaborate stitches lend themselves to wholecloth projects or fairly plain background fabrics, as they may be lost on a busy background. Linear stitches and individual stitches that can be stippled or arranged for texture infill are all useful. Combine fancy stitches with simpler ones, including the basic quilting running stitch. Start and finish by "popping the knot" (see page 110).

318 Thread and fabric contrast

You will want to be able to see your quilting stitches clearly against the background, so the beautiful embroidery patterns are revealed. A contrast between thread and fabric will help you achieve this, in color, tone, or texture. Multicolored threads can shade in and out of the background color or contrast completely. See page 11 for ideas on suitable threads, and experiment with embroidery threads. Sewing some embroidery stitches causes the thread to untwist as you sew, so check your thread and, if necessary, retwist it from time to time as you stitch. Make smaller stitches with finer thread, so the stitches remain well-proportioned and don't look straggly.

FIX IT

319 Thick threads

Some threads will be too thick to stitch with easily. Try couching very thick or fancy textured threads, laying the thread against the fabric and stitching across it, either by hand or machine. Weaker threads, including shiny rayon, can be used for whipped and threaded stitches, as shown here.

320

Stitching variety

Here is a selection of stitches that work well as alternates to running stitch. Other stitches can be researched from embroidery books.

Stem stitch

Stem stitch is a solid outlining stitch that is good for holding the quilt layers together. Holding the thread below the stitching line with the thumb of your non-sewing hand, take a small stitch backward through all the layers, toward the starting point. Repeat the stitch along the line, coming up for each new stitch where the last stitch ends. Hold the thread out of the way at the start of each stitch, as shown.

Single feather stitch

Use single feather stitch for delicate effects. Working toward you, hold the thread down the line and looped to the right. Make a stitch through all the layers to the right of the stitch line, stitching diagonally downward and inward, as shown. Bring the needle up inside the loop. Repeat the stitch, this time sloping to the left of the line. Continue to repeat the first two stitches. Finish with a small stitch over the last loop, as shown.

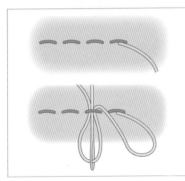

Whipped running stitch

Whipped running stitch is a bold stitch that can use difficult threads for the whipped contrast, as shown above. The running stitches need to be between $\frac{1}{8}$ in and $\frac{1}{4}$ in (3 mm and 6 mm) long. Use a contrasting thread for the whipping. Bring the whipping thread to the front, just below the center of the first running stitch. Pass the eye end of the needle behind each subsequent running stitch in turn, threading in the same direction each time—from top to bottom or from bottom to top.

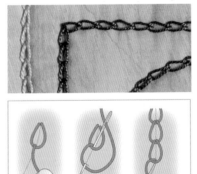

Chain stitch

Chain stitch creates a solid outline, wider than stem stitch. Using the thumb of your non-sewing hand, hold the thread ahead of the starting point, to make a loop. Take the needle back through the starting hole and take a stitch forward through all the layers. Bring the needle up inside the loop, pull through, and immediately form the loop for the next stitch. Repeat along the stitch line. Secure the last loop with a small stitch, as shown. Individual chain stitches, worked like the last stitch, can be worked in a circle to make "lazy daisy" flowers or scattered as an infill.

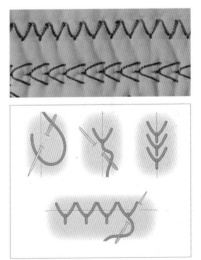

Fly stitch

This stitch can be sewn in horizontal or vertical rows or scattered as a filling stitch. Hold the thread downward and looped to the right. Take the needle in through the right hand side of the line, making a quilting stitch at a downward diagonal. Bring the needle up and into the loop, before taking the needle down and holding the loop in place. Repeat. The length of the holding stitch can be varied.

Corded quilting and trapunto

Corded quilting and trapunto techniques add a more three-dimensional effect to your quilting, by adding extra padding to selected areas. Corded quilting is made by threading yarn between two lines of quilting, while trapunto has extra batting inserted. The techniques may be combined very successfully, as in the French Provençal *boutis* ("stuffing") quilting tradition, and are mostly used for wholecloth quilts.

FIX IT

321 *Yarn not chunky enough?*

"Trapunto" wool yarn is specially made for corded quilting and trapunto padding, but thicker "super chunky" knitting yarns can be substituted. Look for a soft yarn rather than a tightly spun, stringy yarn. Traditional wool will shrink when washed, hence the importance of turning loops. Acrylic yarn does not shrink, so tension loops are not necessary on the back. It makes a good substitute if you intend to wash the quilt frequently, but will melt if pressed. Using colored yarns produces an effect similar to shadow quilting, with touches of pastel color showing through pale fabric. Cotton yarns are available for boutis, or try knitting cottons instead.

322 Corded quilting basics

Cording, also known as Italian quilting, dates back to the seventeenth century, when it was used for bedding and clothing. Designs lend themselves to the parallel lines of stitching required for the cording channels, so knotwork and simple outline designs work best. Use a loosely woven fabric for the backing, like muslin, where the threads can be pushed apart with a large bodkin, enabling you to thread the yarn into the channels.

1 | Trace the design onto your fabric. (Light-colored fabrics are traditionally used, as the pattern is enhanced by the shadows on the quilt, so tracing is easiest.) Pin or baste the two layers together and hand or machine quilt, following the outlines. Lines ¼ in (6 mm) apart are just the right width to take trapunto yarn, without it being too tight or too loose.

2 | Turn the work over, so you are working from the back. Thread the bodkin with yarn. Easing the threads apart in the backing fabric, insert the bodkin and work the yarn through the stitched channel. Bring the needle out of the backing at regular intervals on long lines, leaving a little loop, and leave another tension loop at every corner or change of direction. If you don't leave a loop, your work will pucker up.

3 | Cut the yarn close to the back of the work at the beginning and end, leaving a short tail of yarn outside the backing fabric. Cut the yarns at intersections too. Traditional corded quilting frequently had no additional batting, but you can layer and quilt your panel with extra batting if you wish, using a thin, low loft batting to emphasize the cording. This way, cording can add highlights to a quilted design.

323 Introducing trapunto

Trapunto motifs are outlined with a single line of quilting through the top fabric and backing layer. Additional batting is inserted from the back. Traditionally, this was done in a similar manner to cording, with a loosely woven backing fabric that enabled the quilter to insert the batting. Soft trapunto wool may be worked into the back of the motif in this way, starting by leading the wool into the motif with a bodkin, then pulling more yarn into the motif with the bodkin point. Each section of the design must be stuffed separately.

Most modern quilters stuff trapunto by making a slit in the backing fabric, inserting wisps of stuffing (polyester stuffing is ideal) using a blunt needle, bamboo skewer, or similar, and then stitching the slit closed. This is fine if the trapunto is going to be backed with another fabric but looks unattractive if left exposed.

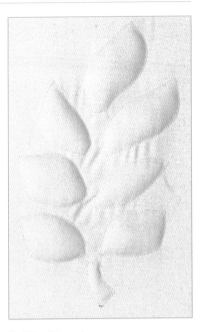

Traditional trapunto produces high-relief three-dimensional effects.

325 Adding extra batting

Another trapunto method is used by machine quilters that can also be applied to hand quilting. An extra layer of batting is basted to the back of the area to be quilted and the excess batting is trimmed away before the quilt sandwich is made. The quilting is completed as normal, except that in the areas with the extra batting you will be stitching through two layers of batting, not one, giving the trapunto effect. It works particularly well if you use a very thin cotton batting for the main batting with a "high loft" polyester batting behind the trapunto areas, or with two layers of polyester. Two layers of cotton batting can be too dense for quilting easily.

1 | Baste the extra batting behind each motif, such as these country chickens. Machine sewing close to the outside of the motif edge will hold the extra layer in place. Use wash-away, water-soluble basting thread on the top of the machine, with light-colored cotton in the bobbin—the bobbin thread will remain in the quilt. (Don't wet this stitching while working on the quilt, as the water-soluble thread will just dissolve.) Carefully trim away the excess batting with a sharp pair of embroidery scissors.

Hand quilting with extra batting adds depth to the hare (see page 23).

TRY IT

324 Machine-flattening a background

Dense machine quilting will successfully flatten a background area and is another way to create a trapunto effect using a low-loft cotton batting and a high-loft polyester one. Make the quilt sandwich with the polyester batting over the whole area of the cotton batting. A quilt with two battings will be bulky to handle on the machine, so try this method for smaller pieces or use it with quilt-as-you-go (see page 116). Machine quilt around the motif, but do not add many machine quilting details in the motif itself. Quilt the background closely with stippling or another dense pattern, squashing down the polyester batting in this area.

2 | Make the quilt sandwich (see page 106). Quilt your project, paying special attention to quilting around the trapunto motifs, in the ditch, to hold the extra batting in place. Densely quilting the background will help to add dimension to the trapunto parts of the design. You may want to separate areas of trapunto in the same motif by quilting through all the layers. These apple and pear motifs have only one piece of batting behind the composite motif, but quilting around the individual shapes gives more definition.

Big-stitch and tying

Bold stitch effects are sometimes just what you want and big-stitch is exactly that. Using thicker threads and larger stitches, this hand quilting technique is a fun finish that can add extra color and texture. Tying is even simpler and may be just what you need with thicker batting.

▓ TRY IT

326 Different materials

Experiment with different kinds of thread to get the effect you want or try tying with silk embroidery ribbon. Buttons can be incorporated into ties, either with the knot on the top or concealed on the back of your work.

329 Threads for big stitches

Thicker threads are necessary to get the big-stitch look—simply making your quilting stitches bigger with a 30s–50s weight thread, will just appear as if your stitches are too large. Longer stitches need chunkier thread to be successful. Embroidery threads, such as fine and medium perlé and coton à broder, are ideal. Cotton sashiko threads (see page 118) are tough and economical to use, as they are sold in much larger skeins.

Many hand-dyed threads are great for big stitch, and multicolored threads add an interesting look. The threads need to be strong and able to withstand the greater wear and tear of being pulled through the quilt and batting, so you may want to test a new thread before embarking on a large project. Since seeing the finished stitches is part of the big-stitch style, choose contrasting threads rather than colors that blend in with the background.

327 The right needles

Embroidery or crewel needles have longer eyes than sharps or betweens, and will be much easier to thread. The eyes are still fairly narrow, so you should have no problems pulling the needle through the quilt sandwich. Try out your chosen needle and thread with the quilt sandwich—if it is difficult to pull the thread through, try changing the size of the needle, which may be too small rather than too large.

330 Big-stitch techniques

Big-stitch is sewn like hand quilting; the stitches are just larger. It may be difficult at first to make larger stitches if you are used to making very small hand quilting stitches, but persevere. Simply using the larger needle will help you make longer stitches. Big-stitch may be easier to sew without using a frame, especially if you are used to lap quilting (see page 111), and the larger needles make the twin thimble quilting technique (page 110) difficult to do. If you are aiming for a very rustic look, it matters less if the stitch length varies. When popping the knot at the start and end of the quilting line (see page 110), a single knot may suffice, as a larger knot in thicker thread may be impossible to pop through the fabric. Keep threads like perlé shorter than 16 in (40.6 cm) so they don't become too worn while stitching or even start to fray.

328 Tying your quilt

Some quilts with very thick batting may be easier to tie than to quilt. You may decide to tie some parts of the quilt as a design feature or because you feel that quilting will detract from the fabric pattern. Tying is a utilitarian form of finishing a quilt but can add textural interest too. With the quilt as flat as possible, take a stitch as shown in the diagram, below, leaving the thread ends long enough to tie in a reef knot. Using several strands together will give a fluffier, tufted effect.

FIX IT

331 Care instructions for gift quilts

If a quilt is to be a gift, it is a good idea to explain to the recipient that the big-stitch quilting or tying is actually the quilting. At least one quilter was surprised to hear that the new owner of the quilt spent a lot of time "removing the basting stitches"!

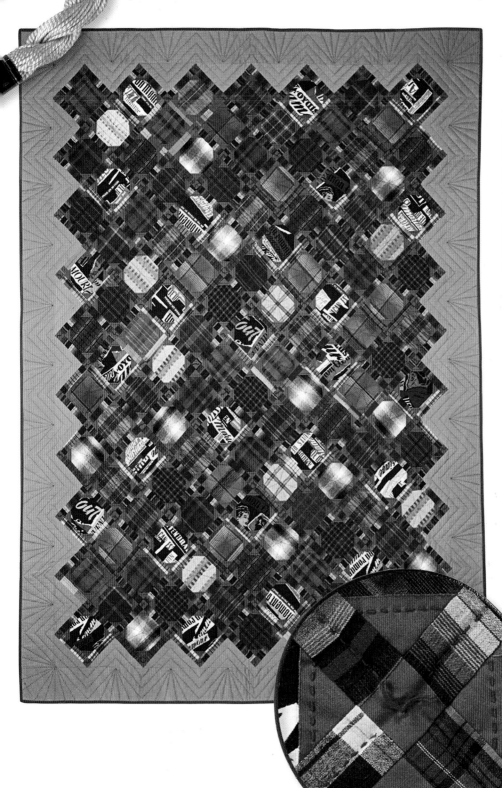

**"Roman Perdu"
(Lost Novel)**
Big-stitch quilting and
tying in the same shade
of deep pink thread
unified this quilt made
with flannel samples.
Because the flannel
was difficult to mark,
strips of masking tape
were used to line up the
simple crossed quilting
pattern. The sashing
posts were tied. Size 85
x 63 in (216 x 160 cm).

Sashing posts
are tied with the
thread doubled.

BINDING AND FINISHING

Take care when binding and finishing your quilt and you will be rewarded with a neat, strong edge.

Types of edge finishes

Binding the quilt edges is a popular way to finish your quilt, either with straight or bias tape. Because you can make binding easily from any patchwork fabric you like, you can coordinate the binding to suit your quilt, framing it with a touch of color. Other ways to finish a quilt include turning in, wrapping, bagging out, and facing (pages 132 and 134), so you can choose the style to complement your quilt.

(pages 132 and 134)

333 Make your own binding

Most commercial bias tape is loosely woven and unsuitable for binding a quilt, so make your own. Binding can be cut on the straight grain, across the fabric, or on the bias. It is sewn to the quilt in two stages—machine or hand sewn to the front of the quilt first, folded over the edge, and hand sewn to the back.

Straight binding has no wastage. Pieces can be cut in long strips and joined on a 45-degree angle. Bias tape may seem less economical, as there will be small triangles left over from the corners of your fabric (see diagram, right)—the ends are already at 45-degree angles, so wastage is about the same. Straight binding cut across the fabric width has a little stretch. Cut with the straight grain, it has no stretch at all.

Binding needs joining so it is long enough to go around the quilt. Use a ¼ in (6 mm) seam on a 45-degree angle, as shown, and press the seam allowance open to reduce bulk. Join straight and bias tape strips in the same way.

Bias tape is stretchy because it is cut on the bias grain, so it is suitable for binding straight and curved edges. Cut the strips diagonally across a square of fabric, as shown. Join pieces together, as above, to make a continuous binding. Handle cut bias edges carefully, so as not to stretch the edges accidentally. Wrap the binding around a piece of cardboard or a cardboard tube to keep it neat.

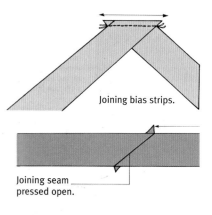

Straight grain

Cutting diagonal bias strips.

Joining bias strips.

Joining seam pressed open.

Checked and printed bindings add visual interest.

336 *Binding problems*

One square yard (or meter) will make 17½ yd (16 m) of 2 in (5 cm) wide binding, either straight or bias. If you don't have quite enough of your chosen fabric for binding, the following ideas will make it go further:

• Try single binding rather than double binding. Single binding is only four times the finished width plus a scant ⅛ in (3 mm), rather than six times the finished width.

• Use smaller seam allowances. A ½ in (1.3 cm) finished binding can be achieved with only ¼ in (6 mm) seam allowances, if the binding edge is set back from the quilt edge by ¼ in (6 mm). Binding strips would be 1⅞ in (4.8 cm) wide, not 2⅛ in (5.4 cm).

• Not adding a little extra to allow for the thickness of the quilt results in tight completed binding—if you do forget this, compensate by setting the edge of the binding a fraction of an inch back from the quilt edge but taking your planned seam allowance. This also allows you to see the edge of the quilt as you stitch the binding, so you should spot any puckers.

• Add pieces of another fabric into the binding, matching the tone rather than the color for plain binding, or make a random patchwork binding from leftover fabrics used for the main quilt.

334

Using double binding

Double binding is wider and is folded and pressed in half along the length before being sewn to the quilt. Set one binding edge fractionally back from the other when pressing, so the extra bulk of the double binding is offset and doesn't make a sudden bump at the binding edge. The double fabric layer gives a firm edge to the quilt. There are no raw edges to deal with once the binding is folded over the quilt edge to be sewn to the back of the quilt. Double binding is bulky and is therefore not suitable for lapped binding with square corners—use mitered corners instead (see page 131).

"Recycled Curves" Plain binding adds a color accent, emphasizing the red silk in the raw-edge appliqué layers. Size 28 in (71 cm).

335

Choosing the right binding

A bed quilt or throw will need a hard-wearing binding, whereas a wallhanging needs a binding that will hang straight.

Bias tape The longest-lasting binding, bias tape wears well because there are many threads in the edge of the binding, rather than just one or two taking all the wear along the length of the edge. It can also flex with the quilt. If your quilt has curved corners, bias tape is essential because straight binding won't lie around a curve.

Doubled bias tape is even more hardwearing, because there are two layers of fabric. There is no need to use bias tape unless you want a particular pattern effect, such as bias stripes along the edges.

Straight binding is good for a wall-hanging, as it will help the edges to hang straight if it is the correct length for the edge of the quilt. Too tight and the quilt will bunch up; too loose and it will ripple. Some quilters like to use bias tape for wall hangings to counteract this, but it should not be a problem if you measure correctly.

Doubled binding provides a stronger option for straight bindings on bed quilts and throws.

The same border and binding fabrics merge together.

Applying lapped binding

Lapped binding is very straightforward to apply and each side of the quilt is sewn separately. Whether you decide to make a lapped binding or to use one of the other binding methods on the following pages, get the quilt ready for the binding in a few simple steps in order to make the binding process easier to do.

▪▪ TRY IT

337 Machine binding

If you want to apply the binding entirely by machine, sew the binding strips to the back of the quilt first, rather than the front. When the binding is folded over the quilt edge ready for stitching, use a narrow zigzag, blind hemstitch (combining straight stitches with zigzags) or a decorative edge stitch to machine sew the binding to the front of the quilt. Make sure the binding edge overlaps the previous stitching line. As the stitches will be visible, bold effects look better. This is a strong method for finishing the binding, perfect for children's and teenagers' quilts.

338 Preparing the quilt for binding

Proper preparation of the quilt edge will make attaching the binding easier and give a better finish. Trim the backing and batting to match the edge of the quilt top, using your rotary cutter, ruler, and mat, checking that the quilt corners are square. Machine or hand sew all around the quilt, ⅛ in (3 mm) from the edge to hold the layers together while binding, using the walking foot for machine quilting. Take measurements for binding through the center of the quilt (not along the edge) for greater accuracy, just like measuring for borders (see page 81). The binding can be machine or hand sewn (in running stitch) for the first step and hand sewn once it is turned over the quilt edge.

339 Matching the binding to your quilt

Not only the fabric but also the binding style can be chosen to complement your quilt design. The square corners of lapped binding look good with strip patchwork like Log Cabin, while mitered binding (see page 131) echoes the diagonal line of mitered borders. You may find it easier to use miters for the corners for narrower bindings, ⅜ in (1 cm) wide or slightly less, as there is very little space to fold in the corners of lapped binding. If your quilt has curved motifs, consider curving the corners to match (see page 130).

"Chō-chō san"
A narrow inner border in bright fabric separates the dark fabrics from the black border in this small wall hanging, as shown in the detail photo. Size 24 x 18 in (61 x 46 cm).

Creating lapped binding

Lapped binding is best made with single binding, to reduce bulk at the corners. Four strips of single binding are required for this method. The binding is usually applied across the top and bottom first and the sides last, so the ends of the top and bottom binding are hidden inside the corners. Cut four binding strips—see Binding problems on page 127 for width information. The length of the top and bottom strips should be the same as the width of the quilt. The length of the side strips should be the same as the length of the quilt plus 1½ in (3.8 cm).

The binding width here echoes the width of the sashing strips, visible back and front in Quilt-as-you-go.

1 | Line up the edge of the binding with the edge of the quilt, pin at right angles to the quilt edge, and stitch with the desired seam allowance for the width of the binding, using the walking foot if machine sewing, and starting and finishing with a few backstitches.

2 | Fold the binding strip over onto the back of the panel, fold the raw edge under, and stitch down to the backing, lining up the fold with the previous stitching line. Make sure the binding is snug around the panel edge. Leave the ends raw.

3 | Bind the sides of the panel as above, but leaving ¾ in (1.9 cm) of binding over each end. Before stitching the binding to the back of the panel, fold these ends over, tucking in the excess fabric and neatening the corners of the binding. Hold the tucked-in fabric in place with a stitch or two at the ends of the binding, and slipstitch the ends of the binding together.

Mitered and curved bindings

Mitered and curved bindings offer two other ways of turning the binding around the quilt corner. Mitered binding is suitable for single and double bindings, as well as straight and bias tape. Curved corners are another option, if your quilt design will suit this style, and these must be made with bias strips.

Curved corners are good for bags, whereas square corners could wear quickly in use.

341 Incorporating curved corners

Depending on the border design, curved corners may suit your quilt. Wide curved corners are a good finish for a bed quilt made to hang over the end of a sofa, as the corners won't trail on the floor. Smaller curves are frequently used for the flaps on satchels and rucksack-style patchwork bags. Any suitably sized circle template can be used to mark the corner curve before stitching around it, just inside the cutting line, and cutting around the curve. If you are not sure if you would like this effect, cut the same size curve out of a sheet of paper and use the remaining paper to mask off the border so you can see how it looks. Use bias tape and ease the binding around the curved corner, without over stretching the binding. If the binding is too tight around the curve, the bound corner will tend to curl up.

▦ TRY IT

342 Curves not squares

Square quilt corners need to be turned neatly to look good. If you feel that lapped corners or miters are going to let your quilt down, try a small curved corner instead. Use a circle with a small diameter as your template. Apply the binding so the corner is flat and well finished.

Mastering mitered binding

Mitered binding is easiest with double binding, best machine sewn for the first steps, as you are stitching through two layers of fabric. Line up the binding along the bottom edge of the quilt, about 12 in (30.5 cm) from the left-hand lower corner of the quilt, setting the raw edges slightly back from the quilt edge. This offsetting avoids too much bulk at the edge of the quilt. You can also see the quilt and both layers of the binding as you pin them together, so you should be able to spot any creases and sort them out. Using the walking foot if you are machine sewing, and your chosen seam allowance, start sewing with a few backstitches about 4 in (10.2 cm) from the corner.

1 | Whatever the finished width of your binding, stop stitching the same distance from the corner. So, for example, if the finished width is ½ in (1.3 cm), end your stitching that far from the corner, finishing with a few backstitches.

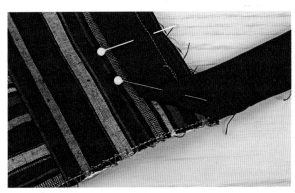

2 | Fold the binding away from the corner, at a 45-degree angle, as shown, to make the miter. Finger press the fold and hold it in place with a pin.

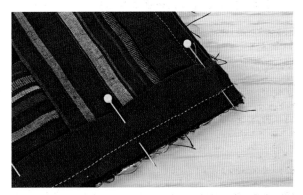

3 | Fold the binding back toward the quilt to make a right angle and pin along the side of the quilt, checking that the length of the binding strip is the same as the length measurement for the quilt. Backstitch up to the top of the fold and stitch the binding to the quilt along the whole side, finishing as for the first miter above. Make all the miters in the same way.

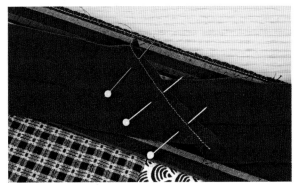

4 | Pin the binding on the fourth side. Cut a 45-degree angle across the end of the 12 in (30.5 cm) length of binding from where you started and overlap this with the other end of the binding, right sides together. With a ¼ in (6 mm) seam allowance, stitch the two ends together and finger-press the seam open. Pin and sew the last section of binding. Fold the binding over and hand sew to the quilt back, as for lapped binding (page 129).

FIX IT

344 *Wavy sides*

Starting the binding on the bottom edge is less obtrusive and means the sides and top of the quilt can have the binding applied in one step, lessening the chance of the quilt rippling if it is hung up. Even if the quilt is to be a bedcover or throw, it pays to do the binding this way—if you decide to display it as a wallhanging or enter it in an exhibition at a later date, any waviness in the side borders would show when it is hung up.

Turned, wrapped, and faced edges

Quilts do not always have to be finished with separate bindings. Turned-in edges, wrapped edges, and facings offer other possibilities. These are not as hardwearing as bound edges but, if used for a bedcover or throw, could be bound at a later date.

FIX IT

345 Neat finishes

Sewing a facing is the easiest way to deal with various fancy edge finishes:

INSERT PIPING For a neatly defined edge, insert piping between the quilt and the facing. It is easy to make your own piping by folding a bias strip around piping cord and stitching close to the cord, using a zipper foot. Insert the piping so the excess bias fabric is sandwiched between the facing and the quilt, stitching close to the piping with the zipper foot once again. Preshrink piping cord before use by soaking it in hot water.

CREATIVE EDGING Sawtooth triangles and prairie points (see page 102) can be sewn all around the quilt edge if they are sandwiched between the quilt and the facing. Sawtooth triangles can be interlocked and adjusted to fit the length of the quilt edge.

ADD FABRIC FRILLS A faced edging allows you to insert a fabric frill. For a narrow frill around 2 in (5 cm) finished depth, allow one-and-a-half times the length of the quilt edge. Gather the edge on the sewing machine, by setting the top tension to zero and using the longest stitch length, distributing the fullness evenly along the edge of the quilt and allowing more fullness to go round corners. This would be an interesting finish for a retro-style quilt.

HANGING ALTERNATIVES Hanging tabs or loops may be inserted into the top edge of a wallhanging as a more decorative hanging alternative to a sleeve (see page 148). Make loops from fabric strips or tubes.

346 Try turned-in edges

Turned-in edges give a traditional finish often seen on old British quilts, frequently machine stitched quite visibly—often rather incongruously, with beautiful hand quilting all over the rest of the quilt! If you plan to use this finishing method, do not quilt right up to the edge or you won't be able to turn the edges in.

Method: Trim the backing to match the quilt top all around. The batting needs to be trimmed back by the same amount you plan to turn under: ½ in (1 cm) or ⅜ in (10 mm) is fine; ¼ in (6 mm) is fiddly to turn, but achievable. If you have striped or checked fabric, use the width of the pattern as a guide. Peel back the top layer of the quilt and trim the batting edge in sections, sliding the edge of the mat between the batting and the backing.

Baste right around the quilt, ¾ in (1.9 cm) from the edge. Beginning with the quilt top, turn under the edge the same distance all around—½ in (1 cm) or whatever allowance you decide to use—and baste ⅛ in (3 mm) from the folded edge, folding and sewing through the top only at this stage. When complete, turn the throw over and repeat with the backing fabric, turning the edge under to match the edge of the folded and tacked top, but this time fold the fabric *over* the batting and baste the backing fabric to the front of the quilt. When the basting is finished, slip stitch by hand all the way around the quilt, stitching the backing to the top. Remove the basting stitches. A single or double row of quilting around the edge is a neat finish.

"Redwork Sampler" by Dot Sherlock
Sawtooth triangles give an interesting finish to this nostalgic quilt, combining old-fashioned red and white prints with redwork embroidery panels. See page 138 for the whole quilt.

Finish with a facing

Facing the edges of the quilt gives an invisible edge finish. The facing is simply a piece of fabric sewn around the edge of the quilt and hemmed to the back.

Method: Trim the quilt ready for applying the facing. If the quilt is small, pin it to the facing fabric, right sides together, and machine sew around the edge using the walking foot and allowing a ¼ in (6 mm) seam allowance. Cut away the center of the facing fabric with a pair of scissors, allowing around 2 in (5 cm) all around the edge for the facing. Trim off the corners within the seam allowance, but do not cut right up to the stitches—only to about ⅛ in (3 mm). Turn the quilt right side out through the gap in the facing. Ease the corners out so they are sharp. Lay the quilt flat, face down, and smooth out the facing. Turn the edges of the facing under, clipping the corners, and hand sew to the back of the quilt.

Keeping the edges neat

From the back, sew right around a faced quilt ⅛ in (3 mm) from the edge with small, neat hand stitches through the backing and seam allowances, only to keep the backing in place. For larger quilts, use strips of fabric for the facing, constructing it like a quilt border (but without a center) before pinning it to the quilt and sewing it as above.

A piped edging is another option for a neat faced-edge finish. Make your own piping to match the quilt fabric.

◾ TRY IT

Faux binding

A faux binding solves a problem if you don't want a separate binding yet want the appearance of a bound quilt (right). The backing fabric is wrapped around the quilt edge and stitched down on the front, as for finishing a mitered binding (see page 131). The backing fabric will be visible all around the quilt, so choose carefully. If you wanted to use the same fabric for backing and binding, but are a few inches short, this is the solution.

• Trim the batting to match the front of the quilt, using the rotary cutting method. Trim the backing fabric to twice the width of the finished wrapped edge, so 1 in (2.5 cm) is sufficient for a ½ in (1.3 cm) "binding" (a). Fold the first backing corner over, shown by the dashed red line (b). Trim off the excess fabric at the corner point beyond the dashed red line. Fold over the edge of the backing along the dashed red line, so the folded edge lines up with the solid red line (c). Stitch the folded edge down and sew the mitered corner, as if dealing with a mitered binding. Stabilize the edge by quilting in the ditch right next to the edge you have just sewn.

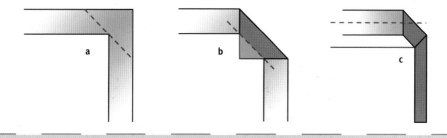

a   b   c

Invisible-edge finish

Ideal for smaller quilts, "bagging out" the backing and the quilt produces a quick and easy edge finish, similar to turned-in edges but simpler to do. No stitching is visible on the right side and the quilt appears to have no edging. Smaller pieces of work are ideal for making cushions, easy with an envelope back.

The bagging-out method

The quilt top, backing, and batting will be basted together in a different order before quilting, so decide if you want to use this finishing method before making the quilt sandwich. The backing and batting need to be slightly larger than the quilt top.

Step 1: Baste the batting to the wrong side of the backing fabric, as if making a quilt sandwich with only two layers, spreading the batting out and laying the backing face down onto it. Baste rather than using pins, which have a tendency to catch on each other when turning the quilt right-side out.

Step 2: Lay the quilt top over the backing and batting sandwich, right sides together with the backing, and smooth it out. Pin and machine sew all around, using a $\frac{1}{4}$ in (6 mm) seam allowance, and leaving a gap, about 10 in (25.4 cm) long, unsewn at the bottom of the quilt.

Trim the backing to the same size as the quilt top. Trim away excess batting from the seam allowance, close to the stitching line. Trim away excess batting across the unsewn gap. Clip the corners, $\frac{1}{8}$ in (3 mm) from the edge, and "bag out"—turn the right side out through the unsewn gap. Smooth the top over the batting and backing, baste the layers together before quilting, and slipstitch the gap closed when complete. Hand-sew around the edge to finish, from the back, taking a short running stitch through the backing and a longer running stitch through the seam allowance inside the edge (about $\frac{1}{2}$ in [3 mm]). Don't let the stitch show on the quilt front. Quilts with irregular edges are easier bagged out than bound, clipping the seam allowance along curves.

"Kesa Quilt"
Bagging out was an appropriate way to finish this quilt, so it looks more like the Japanese monk's kesa patchwork robes that inspired the design, which are finished with a wide border but not bound. Size 71 x 42 in (180.3 x 106.7 cm).

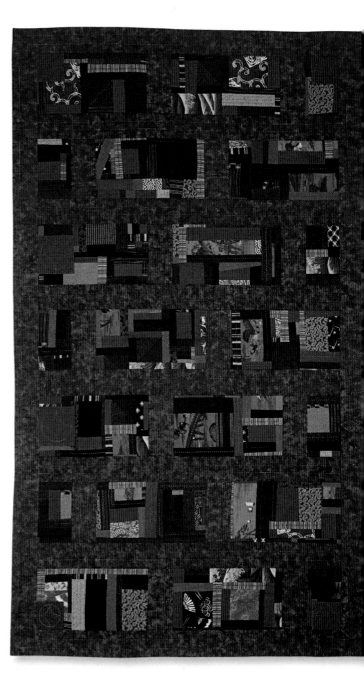

Working with envelope-backed cushions

Patchwork, appliqué, and quilted cushions are always popular, as they are so much quicker to make than a quilt, and make welcome gifts. This is a simple way to make a cushion. The cushion pad is inserted through the back panel overlap. An overlap that is too small won't stay closed (try adding a button closure) but make it too wide and it will be difficult to get the pad through the gap. You will need two pieces of backing fabric the same length as your cushion and 60 to 70 percent of the width for an adequate overlap. The outer back panel edge can be decorated to complement the cushion front. Try simple patchwork for the back panels if you don't have enough of one fabric.

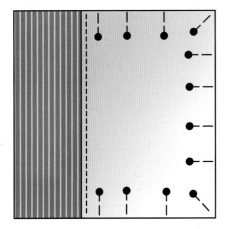

1 | Hem one long edge of each back panel and zigzag or overlock the other edges. Place the patchwork and one of the backing pieces right sides together and pin.

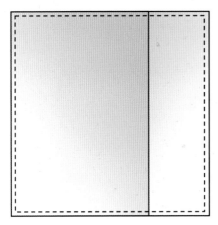

2 | Place the second backing piece right sides together, overlapping the first piece, and pin. Machine-sew around the edge, with a ½ in (1 cm) seam allowance, as shown by the dashed line. Clip the corners, as described opposite, and turn right side out. Insert the cushion pad through the gap.

**"Crazy Cushions"
by Jenny Hewer**
These cushions have envelope backs but are bound like quilts.

FIX IT

352 *Narrow back panels*

Add a button fastening to the overlap if you like—a solution if your back panels aren't wide enough and the back might gape. Stitch the buttonholes by hand or machine before sewing the backing panels in place, and add the buttons when the cushion cover is complete.

Labeling your quilt

Adding a label to your quilt is the finishing touch. How many vintage quilts are now anonymous, because we don't know when, where, and by whom they were made? A securely attached label is a message for the future as well as identifying the quilt today. It can also help identify your quilt if it is lost or stolen.

353 Information to include

The amount of information on the quilt label is up to you, but typically would include the information described below.

354 Using ready-made labels

Ready-made quilt labels have border designs and motifs that may echo the design on your quilt, as well as space for you to add your information. You can print your own labels direct from the computer (see page 26). Use a word processing program to write your label or use one of the dedicated quilt label programs now available. Creating labels on the computer means you can incorporate photos too.

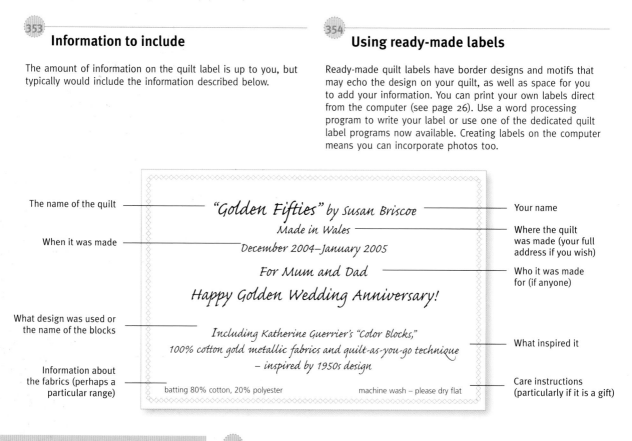

The name of the quilt — *"Golden Fifties"* by Susan Briscoe — Your name

When it was made — *Made in Wales* — Where the quilt was made (your full address if you wish)

December 2004–January 2005

For Mum and Dad — Who it was made for (if anyone)

Happy Golden Wedding Anniversary!

What design was used or the name of the blocks — *Including Katherine Guerrier's "Color Blocks,"*

100% cotton gold metallic fabrics and quilt-as-you-go technique — What inspired it

– inspired by 1950s design

Information about the fabrics (perhaps a particular range) — batting 80% cotton, 20% polyester

machine wash – please dry flat — Care instructions (particularly if it is a gift)

TRY IT

355 Shaped labels

Shaped labels may be appropriate for your quilt. Triangular labels will fit neatly into a corner. You can use the outline of an appliqué motif for your label. A simple heart is also a popular shape.

356 Designing labels

Most labels are made separately and appliquéd to the back of the quilt. They are usually positioned in a corner. Straight edges can be simply pressed in place before you attach the label, while fancy shapes can be appliquéd (see needleturn appliqué, page 91). Hand sew the label securely to the back of the quilt, making sure you stitch only through the quilt backing.

The simplest labels can be made from a plain calico, with the information handwritten neatly with an acid-free, permanent marker or fibertip pen. Some inks will require pressing to set the color, so they don't run if washed or wetted. Stabilize the label by ironing a piece of freezer paper onto the back before you start. Lightly mark pencil lines on the fabric if you want to keep your writing straight. Practice writing on fabric until you are happy with the results, as it feels different to writing on paper. Try word processing programs to make labels for printing from your computer (see page 26).

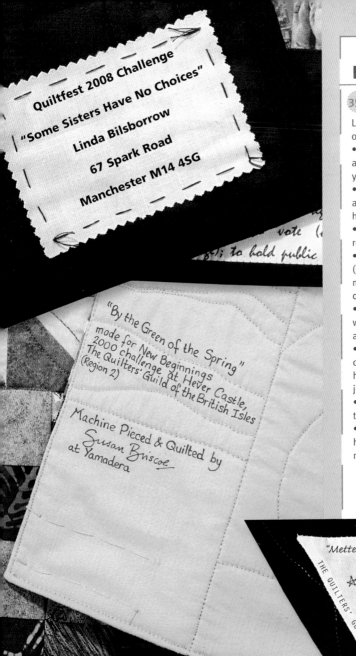

Quiltfest 2008 Challenge
"Some Sisters Have No Choices"
Linda Bilsborrow
67 Spark Road
Manchester M14 4SG

"By the Green of the Spring"
made for New Beginnings
2000 challenge at Hever Castle,
The Quilters' Guild of the British Isles
(Region 2)

Machine Pieced & Quilted by
Susan Briscoe
at Yamadera

FIX IT

358 *Worried about losing your quilt?*

Labeling your quilt will help identify it should it be lost or stolen. Try the following ideas:
• Identify your quilt with your surname, house number, and zip code if you do not feel comfortable putting all your home address information on the quilt label.
• Label the quilt in a corner before attaching the binding, and overlap the label with the binding, so the label is harder to remove.
• Piece the label into the backing fabric, so it cannot be removed without leaving a gap, and quilt through it.
• Bond the label to the backing fabric before quilting (see fused appliqué, page 86). Because the bonding material stiffens the fabric making it difficult to hand quilt, use this method for machine-quilted items only.
• Label your quilt straight onto the backing fabric, writing the label by hand with a suitable marker on a light-colored part of the backing.
• Add extra labeling for security by hiding your contact details somewhere on the quilt, such as under the hanging sleeve for wallhangings or exhibition entries, or just under the binding.
• Microchipping a quilt (like pet ID chips), is a new way to identify the quilt.
• Back up the quilt's identity on the label by keeping high-quality photographs of the front and back, which may include photos of the quilt being made.

"Mettez un grain de cette dans votre quilt"

THE QUILTERS' GUILD OF THE BRITISH ISLES NO 30731

✳ *Solstice* ✳

MADE BY
Susan Briscoe ✳
AT
YAMADERA
NORTH WALES

FEBRUARY 2001

✳

This label was shaped to fit a triangular quilt.

357

Embroidering labels

Embroidered labels are an elegant, traditional solution but take longer to make. Hand or machine embroidery is an option. Some computerized machines include embroidered alphabets and can be programmed to stitch words and phrases. Free-motion quilting, with a stabilizer behind the label, is another way to make a label. Cursive writing is easiest to do in this case.

QUILT GROUP FUN

Quilting groups are a great way to make friends with others who share your sewing interests and enjoy working together.

Groups and projects

Many quilting friends meet on a regular basis as a group, ranging from half a dozen quilters getting together at each other's homes, right through to large groups who meet at a community center or hall. If you don't know of any quilt groups in your area, ask at local quilt and craft stores, contact your national quilting guild or association, or see if friends are interested in setting one up.

359 Quilting community

As well as simply getting together to enjoy your individual patchwork and quilting projects, quilting friends can be a great source of support and encouragement. There are many ideas for projects that can involve the whole group, helping your skills and ideas to develop. Just getting together with other quilters can help with ideas and solutions. As well as more conventional groups, there are now online groups and communities too.

"Poole" by Pat Morris
The original appliqué design on this table runner was inspired by vibrant Poole ceramics. The all-over stippled background was suggested by other group members as the perfect finishing touch. Size 14 x 35 in (36 x 89 cm).

FIX IT

360 Different sized blocks

No matter what size block you choose, there will be some variation in size, due to different quilters and even different sewing machines. Putting the blocks together with borders will help make them fit.

361 Making charity quilts

Some local and national charities collect and distribute quilts for sick children or other vulnerable people. Many quilt groups make quilts for charities like these and may organize a special patchwork day to make quick quilt tops that can be quilted with simple designs. Because the patchwork doesn't have to be complicated, an event like this would be good if you have a lot of beginners in the group.

"Red work Sampler" by Dot Sherlock and Jean Jackson
Two friends took part in a red work challenge, embroidering some blocks and piecing others from vintage from red and white fabrics. The resulting quilts show how the same blocks can be made into two very different quilts. Sizes 58 x 50 in (147 x 127 cm) and 54 x 42 in (137 x 107 cm).

"Summer Boromono" by Charlotte Turner
A themed fat quarter bundle makes a good choice for a quick quilt made at a group workshop. The design focuses on a sewing and cutting technique rather than measured blocks, so no two blocks are alike. See "Boromono" on page 58 for another version of this panel. Size 22 x 32 in (56 x 81 cm).

362
Organize a round robin

A round robin is best for a group of quilters of a similar standard. Everyone makes the quilt center to a particular pattern or size and passes their work on to the next quilter, who will add a border before giving it to the next person to add another. Three or four borders are usual. The person who made the center usually keeps the top and borders should be added in keeping with the center. Most round robin quilts are medallion format, although you could try a one-of-a-kind arrangement like the quilt on page 30. A simple theme is usually chosen for each border, such as squares, curves, triangles, or appliqué.

TRY IT

363 **Block swaps**

Everyone in a group makes a set of blocks to a particular size and exchanges them with other members, so each quilter has a complete set of blocks. This can get rather complicated if each quilter wants a different color scheme, so decide on a color scheme you will all use. Quilters can choose to make a particular block, so unless you are all of a similar standard, include some easier blocks for less experienced quilters to make. If everyone makes a different block, you can all make sampler quilts.

364 **Quilt challenge**

Set a theme and invite everyone to make a project. These don't have to be large quilts—smaller projects are usually more popular. A challenge can be based around a block pattern, some quilts from the "Sister's Choice" block challenge are shown on pages 32 and 42. If your group includes beginners and more experienced quilters, a color theme (such as "black and white"), a particular fabric (perhaps a "difficult" fabric or a specific range), a word (like "travel," "spring," or "countryside") or a phrase (something like "butterflies and blooms," "winter warmers," or "chasing rainbows") may be a better choice for your challenge, as they can be interpreted with techniques of varying skill levels. You can set a size restriction too, which is useful if you plan to show the quilts together at an exhibition.

365 **Mystery quilt**

A mystery quilt, like the round robin, is often a medallion design, but not always. The instructions are given out a part at a time, so the quilters don't know exactly what the finished quilt will look like. Instructions can be very specific, with block sizes, complete patchwork instructions and appliqué patterns, or they can refer to a technique. The fun is in not knowing what will come next and being surprised by the finished quilt. It certainly helps to have a good design, as an unattractive quilt would make a bad subject for a mystery project.

Making a group quilt

Many groups make a quilt together at some stage, and it is a popular way to make a quilt for charity fundraising, usually via a raffle or prize draw. With careful planning and coordination, your group can produce an attractive and well-made quilt that will delight any raffle winner.

TRY IT

366 Finding the right color scheme

You can organize the color scheme in various ways to ensure success. Here are some suggestions:

• Give each quilter a piece of the most colorful fabric and ask them to coordinate their blocks around those colors, choosing all the other fabrics themselves. You will be surprised just what colors some of them will spot in that fabric—one may notice a tiny amount of orange or lime green, so be prepared for some unexpected color combinations in their blocks.

• Ask quilters to bring a fat quarter each that will coordinate with the fabrics already chosen. Divide the fat quarters into squares or strips as appropriate for the block design and redistribute the fabrics among the group, so everyone has a mixture of fabrics for their block.

• Choose a monochromatic color scheme, such as black and white or shades of blue. Liven this up with a complementary color.

• Making six or more extra blocks gives the project coordinator options when combining the blocks for the quilt, with some left over for cushions, bags, or other smaller items that will make good second and third prizes.

367 Organizing the team

While the decisions about a group quilt project need to be made by the group as a whole, one person or a small group need to take charge and coordinate the quilt from start to finish. This should include the person who is going to collect the blocks, assemble the quilt top, organize the quilting, sew the binding, and make the arrangements for the raffle, to name just a few stages.

368 Choosing a pattern

The quilt design needs to be one that many people can work on at the same time, so a block-based quilt design tends to be the obvious choice. As you will be selling tickets to people who don't quilt and probably don't know much about quilting, select a simple but effective design that will appeal to different tastes. If your quilt group has beginners who would like to take part, choose a block that they will be able to make too.

369 Color scheme and fabrics

The blocks will need to coordinate to make an attractive quilt. Make clear to everyone that only good quality cotton quilting fabrics must be used. Select one or two fabrics as a starting point, such as the fabric to be used for the border, the sashing (if there is any), or the background. A popular color scheme, rather than something really offbeat, will probably help you sell more tickets.

Quilt coordinated by Deborah Gordon, machine quilted by Linda Paris
The wavy striped border fabric was the starting point for color coordinating this foundation-pieced quilt made by Wrexham Quilting Circle in 2006. Each quilter made two blocks. Size 58 x 43 in (147 x 109 cm).

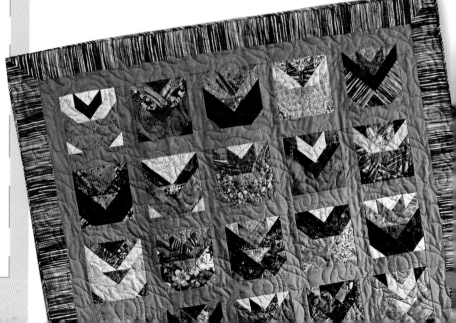

379
Coordinating the effort

Check that everyone knows what they are doing to make their block or blocks. Distribute a handout with all the information they need, such as a cutting list, block construction, and finished size—word of mouth instructions tend to get forgotten along the way. If you foresee any problems, suggest a demonstration or workshop to make the blocks, where everyone can help each other. Allow everyone a reasonable length of time to make their blocks—three or four months is ample time.

371
Arranging the blocks

From the earliest stage, you will need to have a rough plan of the quilt. Once all the blocks are completed, get the group involved with arranging the blocks until everyone is happy with the result. Use a digital camera to photograph each arrangement. The photos can be printed out to help the group decide on the best layout. Once agreed, the quilt top needs to be assembled. It is more likely to be a success if one person sews the blocks together, so all the seam allowances are the same. Add the border if there is one and prepare the top for quilting.

372
Getting it quilted

Unless you have a very enthusiastic expert hand quilter or skilled machine quilter with lots of time to spare, or the timescale for producing the quilt is very long indeed, professional quilting is the best option. A long-arm quilting service (see page 114) will be able to give your quilt the quality finish required to sell those raffle tickets.

373
Raffling the quilt

Check with your local authority or council about the license or permits necessary to raffle the quilt. In many areas, it is possible to run a raffle without any permits if the tickets are sold to paying visitors in one venue on one day. Although getting a license or permit will cost money, there may be advantages of being able to sell over a longer time period and in more than one place. Once the raffle is drawn, remember that you will need to deliver the quilt to its new owner.

Detail of "African Quilt" by the Tuesday Strippers and Alsager Ps and Qs
Made using the same design as "Roman Perdu" (page 125) but with African fabrics, to raise funds for a children's charity.

"Corner in the Cabin" by Dot Sherlock
The quilter enjoyed making her blocks so much, she made another quilt using Corner in the Cabin blocks, setting herself the challenge of working with a color she disliked—lime green. The bright citrus colors make the quilt sing. Size 50 in (127 cm) square.

SHOWS AND EXHIBITIONS

If you and members of your quilt group have produced a fabulous collection of quilts, you will want to share them with others—shows and exhibitions are the places to do just that.

Your quilt group's exhibition

Many quilt groups stage their own exhibitions, for one day, a weekend or longer, some as a regular or even annual event. From the smallest show just for friends right through to month-long events open to the public, smaller quilt shows are a great way to share your enthusiasm and enjoyment of quilting with a wider group of people.

375 What quilts to show and where to exhibit

Obviously your exhibits will include quilts, and plenty of them. If this is your first exhibition, your quilters can delve into their collection, but if you plan to hold an annual or biennial exhibition it is a good idea to keep the selection fresh by accepting only work finished in the previous one or two years. You can include large and small works, bags, cushions, and other items as well as full-size bed quilts, if you have the space to display them.

If you meet in a community center, church hall, or similar venue, it may be suitable for an exhibition. Local museums, libraries, and art galleries are other possibilities. A building that is already in regular public use is best, as you will have fewer extra regulations to follow and there is already likely to be car parking, public transportation access, or both.

Quilts displayed between the pews at the annual Gresford Craft Group exhibition in the fifteenth-century All Saints' Church, Gresford, UK.

376 Organizing your exhibition

Arranging everything for an exhibition is too much work for one person, so set up a group or committee. Different people can be responsible for different aspects of organization. Make use of quilters' existing skills and contacts. Hold regular meetings to check on progress and discuss any problems that crop up. Areas to cover include:
• Insurance, permits, and licenses—make sure you comply with local and national laws and regulations in all that you do.
• Publicity—flyers and posters, the local press, TV, and radio.
• Fundraising—raffle, for which you may or may not need a license (check how you are affected by local legislation).
• Refreshments and facilities—tea and coffee with snacks will be very welcome.
• Quilt store—invite your local quilt store to have a trading booth.

377

Tracking the exhibits

Getting everything together can be one of the trickier parts of preparation, as a large number of quilts take up more space than you might imagine. If you can arrange for the quilters to bring their quilts on the morning of your setting-up day and to collect them at the end of the exhibition, it will save a lot of storage problems.

Ask everyone to fill in a form, giving details of their exhibit, several months before the exhibition. You will want to know the title, the type of item, the hanging system (such as sleeve or loops) if applicable, its size, and some information about the design, technique, what it was made for, and so on. Use this information to create your catalog, or put the sheets in a folder for reference during the exhibition. Also ask for the replacement value, based on the cost of the materials and the time taken to make the item (you will need this information for your insurance forms).

It is very important that you know exactly what you have got and to whom it belongs, so ask for labels on everything as well. Set up a checking-in system for the quilts and issue receipts. You don't want to mislay someone's quilt, give two cushions back to the wrong quilters at the end of the exhibition, or be accused of having lost an item that was listed in the catalog but never brought to the exhibition. Use the information forms to sign the work in at the start of the setting up day and out again when the exhibition is over.

378

The catalog

A catalog is a good idea, listing the names of the makers and their quilts, as visitors will want to know about the exhibits. If you give each quilter a letter or number, working alphabetically by last name, you can simply label each exhibit with a small tag which visitors can cross-reference with the catalog. Depending on the size of your exhibition and the anticipated number of visitors at any given time, you can print the catalogs as small booklets for sale or loan and return or assemble half a dozen catalogs in ringbinders for visitors to carry around.

379

After the exhibition

Take down the quilts and other items and group them by maker. Arrange for the quilters to collect quilts an hour or so after the exhibition closes, as you will need time to take it down. Operate a sign-out system, so everything is accounted for.

380

Running the exhibition

You will need plenty of volunteers to manage the exhibition, sell tickets, help visitors, and maintain security. A kitchen team will be needed to serve refreshments and clean up. Designate some "quilt angels" to wear white cotton gloves to handle quilts on behalf of visitors or, if the displays are very secure, provide white gloves for exhibitors to use. Make sure no one can pull a quilt stand over if you do this. Pay attention to security while setting up and taking down the exhibition, as this is a very vulnerable time for things to go missing.

Organize quilters to demonstrate various quilting skills, as visitors are always interested to find out how quilts are made.

TRY IT

381 Making the most of the display

Quilts can be displayed in many ways in an exhibition—on quilt stands and tabletops, or over chairs, drying racks, and quilt frames. Quilts that will be hung must be supplied with a 4 in (10 cm) hanging sleeve already securely attached. Try displaying items themed by color or style, while grouping challenge and workshop projects together. Unless you are exhibiting in a gallery, you are unlikely to be able to attach items to the walls with screws or nails, so it is best to go for freestanding displays. Quilts can be accessorized with items like vintage sewing machines (needles removed) or dry floral displays. Resist the temptation to accessorize with small or valuable items that might be broken, lost, or stolen. For similar reasons, display small items near to the managers' main table or in display cases. Quilts are very tactile items and you need to have plenty of "Please do not touch" signs on display to protect the quilts from curious fingers. A small "touchable" display is a good compromise.

Visiting a large show

You may have visited smaller local quilt shows but visiting a large regional, national, or international show for the first time is a memorable experience. Prepare to be almost overwhelmed with ideas and inspirations as you view the incredible array of quilts on display, take workshops with expert teachers, and enjoy shopping with the dealers.

382 Finding out about exhibitions

The larger quilt shows will be advertised in quilting magazines in the preceding months. Ads will give details of the show, as well as information on where to buy tickets, and how to find the venue. There are travel companies offering day trips to the largest shows or, for international shows, you can book the quilting version of a package holiday. Local quilt groups often run bus trips to quilting exhibitions, so ask around. Even if your group doesn't run a trip, you may be able to join in with another group. There is often a discount if you buy your ticket in advance.

383 Preparing for the day

Most quilters look forward to attending a quilt show but don't neglect some advance preparation. Make sure you have the following if you want to store and enjoy the exhibits without hassles:
• **Cash** Even if you do not intend to buy anything, you may want some refreshments. Don't rely on quilt stores accepting credit cards.
• **Check book** Smaller stores and demonstrators still accept checks.
• **Camera** A digital camera with a large memory card is easiest. Check that batteries are charged and take spares.
• **Notebook and pencil** Squared paper is best for making quick notes about inspirational designs.
• **Fabric swatches, threads, and so on** Take any you are hoping to match.
• **Shopping list** You probably won't stick to it, but it is frustrating to come home without the very item you wanted most.

384 Tips for maximum enjoyment

• **Dress for comfort** The temperature in the venue can vary from chilly to overpoweringly warm, depending on the time of day, the numbers of quilters, and the efficiency of the air conditioning. Wear layers so you can stay comfortable. It may not be the place to wear that quilted coat you made, although a light quilted vest can ward off air conditioning chill. Wear comfortable shoes as you will be doing a lot of walking. Take a bottle of water so you don't get dehydrated and a snack or packed lunch if you don't want to wait in line.
• **Be prepared** Pack your show supplies the day before, so you are not racing around at the last minute looking for things. A backpack or large bag over your shoulder is a good way to carry all your supplies, with your money and credit cards in a smaller pouch or purse. If you use a backpack, be sensitive to other visitors and try to avoid stepping back into someone with your extra depth! Some quilters like to take shopping bags on wheels or even small wheeled suitcases, but do check in advance— roller bags are banned at some shows as other visitors have been injured by careless use. If they are allowed, be careful in crowded aisles.

385 At the show

• **Catalogs** You will be able to buy a catalog at the entrance to most shows. This lists all the quilts and quilt-makers in the exhibition, plus contact details for the traders and demonstrators. You can use it to make notes about the quilts you like and for dealers' contact information and website addresses. Put your name and brief contact details inside, in case you put it down on a booth and forget it—then there's a chance it (and your notes inside) may be returned.
• **Workshops** Many shows have a variety of workshops on offer with well-known tutors and quilt-book authors, including one-hour workshops, half days, or full days. Obviously you would not want to do a full-day workshop if you are only attending for one day, but a taster session might be fitted in. Check whether workshops have to be booked in advance or can be signed up for on the day. Exhibitions offering advance sign up nearly always sell out before the exhibition opens, although it may be worth checking on the day in case any tickets are returned. If the workshops can be signed up for on the day, go straight to the sign up desk on arrival, as many will sell out in the first half-hour. A workshop in the middle of the show can provide a welcome break as well as being an enjoyable introduction to a new technique.
• **Shopping** Make time for some shopping. Many quilt stores will be attending larger shows and, other than going to their store, this may be your best chance to see their fabrics. "Show specials" are frequently offered and you can make significant savings overall, recouping the cost of your ticket if you shop wisely.

386
Photography

Most shows still allow photography. Please respect signs requesting you to only use your photos for your personal enjoyment and not for commercial use. This includes putting up dozens of photos online. Where there are "no photography" signs, abide by the rules. At the beginning and end of the day the show will be quieter and this can be the best time to revisit quilts you'd like to take a photo of, without having to wait for other visitors to move out of your way. If you are using a digital camera, select the highest resolution settings and take additional detail photos. It is frustrating to want to see stitching detail in a photo only to zoom in and see lots of pixels. Take a photo showing the quilt number label so you can refer back to the catalog later.

FIX IT

387 *Unsure of the shopping etiquette?*

A quilt show is a busy shopping environment, so observe the following:

• Remember that the exhibition environment is full of temporary structures. While these will have been constructed as solidly as possible, it is best not to lean on shelves, tables, or quilt display stands.

• Demonstrators and dealers are usually in a very confined space. Please don't misuse their display area by putting your bags on top of their stock while you rummage for your purse. The next person who wants that fat quarter might find your bag has made a dirty mark on it. Likewise, don't unnecessarily mess up those fat quarter boxes, as the next quilter might miss the fabric they are searching for, and the dealer will have to tidy up after you.

• Respect "no photography" signs on dealers' and demonstrators' displays. Unlike the quilts in the exhibition, whose makers have consented to photography (if permitted), quilts and other designs on sales displays are commercial samples and you would be trying to steal someone's design if you were to take a photograph.

Quilts are hung on specially designed display systems, with the catalog identification number clearly displayed next to each exhibit.

Entering a competitive show

You don't have to be an expert quilter to enter your quilt in a major quilt exhibition. Some shows have categories and prizes for beginners, so quilters of all abilities can enter. The thrill of seeing your quilt being admired with hundreds of others is not to be missed.

■ TRY IT

388 Challenge yourself

Quilt challenges are popular and usually have a set theme. They are frequently themed around fabric ranges, with requirements that you include a certain percentage of the challenge fabric in your quilt, so make sure you do. It is a good excuse to have fun with a specific fabric range. Ingenious interpretations of the theme subject and original design dominate challenge quilts. Pay special attention to the requirements for challenge categories, which can be very particular regarding the size of the completed quilt.

389 Entry forms and rules

Quilting magazines carry details of forthcoming competitive quilt exhibitions, with information about where to obtain entry forms or collect entry forms at quilt shows. Typically, there will be one entry form per show, covering all the different categories. You will need one entry form per quilt. There will be an entry fee, sometimes offset with a free show ticket. Some shows operate a pre-entry registration system, so check if there is more than one stage for the application returns. There will be a deadline for returning the forms. Don't forget!

• **Read the entry form thoroughly** Note the different categories and decide the most appropriate for your quilt. Categories may be listed by style (traditional, contemporary, innovative), quilt type (bed quilt, large wallhanging, cushion), theme categories, or a combination of these (traditional bed quilt, themed wallhanging). A professionally quilted piece should be entered as a two person quilt and the quilter credited. A quilt in the wrong category may be hung but disqualified from judging if it doesn't meet the requirements.

• **Consult the organizers** If you are not sure which category to enter, ask. Some shows allow quilts to be moved to a more appropriate category, but this is rare. While some shows are juried from photographs, others are open to anyone who enters. Some exhibitions exclude quilts that have previously been exhibited in competitive exhibitions, so check carefully.

• **Check the boxes** Many shows offer additional prizes across the whole range of quilts, such as a prizes for various techniques (quilting, patchwork, appliqué), use of color, scrap quilt, sampler quilt, and the like. To be considered for these prizes, make sure you check any boxes relating to techniques used.

"Shalimar"
Made for the Hoffman Challenge (UK) themed quilt contest in 2001 and including the challenge fabrics, fine metallic cord was couched around appliqué motifs and in the ditch along patchwork seams after machine quilting. Hand quilting and sparkly beads add to the effect, inspired by Kay Nielsen's book illustrations. Size 39½ in (1 m) square.

THE SPRING 2009 QUILT FESTIVAL CHALLENGE THEME: "FUN WITH FOLK-ART"

Kindly sponsored by Makower UK,
118 Greys Road, Henley On Thames,
Oxon, RG9 1QW.
Tel. 01491 579727
Email: info@makoweruk.com
Web: www.makoweruk.com
Your opportunity to participate and win 50 fat quarters of fabulous fabrics and a 1 year subscription to Fabrication Quilting For You Magazine.

Sewing
Any original wall hanging, quilting, appliqué or creative on the theme "FUN WITH FOLK-ART" to measure 24" (60cm) wide. Add a sleeve 3" (7.5cm) deep to the top back for hanging.

Entering
Four weeks (or sooner) before the Quilt Fair, send the completed photograph of your quilt for £10.00 (this fee). Then deliver your quilt to the venue by hand or by post to the working days before the opening, delivering with your receipt.

Accepting
The Organizers reserve the right entries are accepted. Every effort entries may not be...

Ret...
Quilts...
On...
by...

ENTRY FORM

390 Entering your quilt

- **Title** You will need to give your quilt a title, even if it is something simple like "Traditional Nine Patch" or "Untitled No.1."
- **Description** Write a short description of your quilt, keeping to the word-count specified. Explain why you used a particular fabric, design, or technique. If you have used a published pattern or adapted a design from a book, say so. Judges have a sound knowledge of the current quilting scene and deliberate plagiarism will be spotted. If you have adapted a published design and used it in your own way, this can be evaluated. Mention any design inspirations, including non-quilting design sources.
- **Images** Many show organizers now request photographs of your quilt, to help with identification purposes. Juried exhibitions used to request slides but many now accept high-resolution digital photographs, including detail photographs, which the judges use to select quilts in advance.

391 The judging process

Quilts are judged before the show opens to the public, often the day before. At this stage, the entries are anonymous, identified only by number. Judging is carried out by a team of experienced quilt judges. The one exception to this rule is the Visitors' Choice category, which is based on visitors' votes for the most popular quilt.

Each section usually has several judges. A points marking system is widely used, with the judges working independently and the points collated at the end of the session. The judges do not confer.

Points may be awarded for design, technique, materials, and use of color and finish. Challenges and themed categories will have extra sections relating to the theme chosen.

All the information you provide will be available to the judges, apart from anything which identifies you as the quilt-maker, including your name, address, and information you may include in the quilt description, like your quilt group's name.

392 Winning

Which quilt wins depends on the others in the competition, not on its individual merits alone. A quilt that didn't win any award at one show may win Best of Show at another. It is futile to enter a show expecting to win a prize, as you will almost certainly be disappointed. Prizes vary from show to show and from one category to another, and include perpetual awards (trophies which are usually held for a year before being returned, including silver cups), rosettes, various trophies that the winners keep, fabric bundles, books, vouchers for quilt stores, sewing machines, and cash prizes.

FIX IT

393 Dropping points?

Many otherwise excellent quilts lose points for "finish," and a point or three makes all the difference for a winning quilt. Your quilt should be clean and well presented. Ask yourself the following questions:
- *Does the quilt hang straight?* A wall hanging that looks baggy or crooked will lose points, although judges may be more lenient for bed quilts. Make sure the hanging sleeve is sewn correctly.
- *Is the binding well sewn?* It should have neat corners, tidy stitching, and be neither too tight nor too loose.
- *Are there loose threads or basting threads showing?* Tidy any loose threads.
- *Can you see the quilt markings?* Try to remove them.
- *Are there hairs or lint on the quilt?* Pet hairs can be a problem. Use a lint roller or a rolled up piece of sticky tape to remove hairs and lint from your quilt.

Preparing your exhibition quilt

Careful preparation will ensure your quilt looks its best in the exhibition. By packing the quilt carefully you can reduce the risk of creasing.

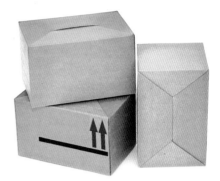

394 Make a hanging sleeve

Your quilt will need a hanging sleeve made to the correct size, usually between 4 and 4½ in (10 and 11.5 cm) deep, to take the wooden lath that will be used to hang the quilt. Details of the minimum depth will be included on the entry form. Narrower sleeves may not be deep enough for the laths used by the exhibitors, even if you have the quilt hung up at home. A tubular hanging sleeve is best—the lath will be completely encased and won't be in contact with the back of the quilt, so there is no chance of accidental damage as the quilt is hung.

Step 1: Cut a strip of cotton twice the desired depth plus a ½ in (1 cm) seam allowance, and as long as the width of the quilt. Turn under a small hem at each end. Fold the strip in half down its length and machine sew to complete the sleeve. This seam will stay on the outside of the sleeve.

Step 2: With the top of the quilt laid out flat and straight, pin the top edge of the sleeve across the top of the quilt, with the seam turned to the back of the sleeve—½ to ¾ in (1 to 1.9 cm) from the top edge is adequate, so it won't show above the top of the quilt when it is hung (below). Hand-sew the sleeve securely to the back of the quilt, stitching through the backing but not through the front of the quilt. Secure the ends.

Step 3: Pin and sew the bottom edge of the sleeve to the quilt, rolling the edge up toward the top of the quilt by about ½ in (1 cm), so there is extra fullness across the outside of the sleeve to accommodate the hanging lath. The quilt will hang without a bump across the top. If the quilt is going to be displayed only once, for a few days, long running stitches close to the edge are adequate. If the quilt may be going on tour, hem the sleeve to the back more securely, checking that the quilt hangs straight first and adjusting the sleeve if necessary.

395 Hanging and blocking your quilt

If you can, check that the quilt will hang straight once the hanging sleeve is sewn, by trying it out on a quilt frame (if you have one) or hanging it up at home before packing it. Some quilters like to block their quilts for a really good finish. You need enough space to lay the quilt out flat for several days to do this. On a sheet on a carpet is ideal, because the quilt edges can be pinned into the carpet. Ease the quilt square and pin on its edges. If you are certain that none of the fabrics or threads will run, cotton quilts may be sprayed lightly with purified water using a plant mister. Don't make the quilt too wet, just slightly damp. Cover with another sheet and leave for several days to dry out. The quilt will have set to shape. If you do not have the space to block a quilt, simply hanging it may help.

396 Exhibition labels

You will be sent an exhibition label to attach to the back of the quilt. Follow the instructions and make sure it is on the correct side, to help the hanging team. Low-tack self-adhesive labels may be stuck to the back of your quilt without leaving a residue, but baste the label to the quilt if you prefer.

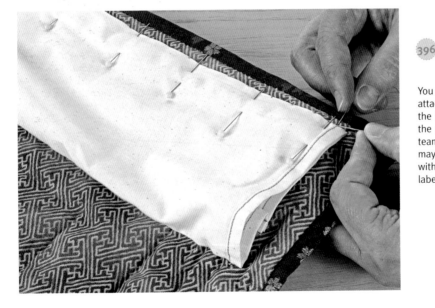

"Images of the Orient"
by Diane Abram
As points are usually awarded for finish, pack carefully so your quilt arrives in perfect condition to hang well and score those extra vital points. Machine appliqué and quilting. Size 46 in (117 cm) square.

397
Packing the quilt

If the quilt isn't too large, rolling the quilt is the best way to pack it. With the right side of the quilt on the outside of the roll, creases will be minimized. Rolling the quilt with the right side inside will add creases. Use a sturdy cardboard tube cut slightly longer than the width of the quilt. The tubes from the insides of carpet rolls are good if you can get them, while giftwrap tubes are fine for smaller quilts. Start rolling at the top of the quilt and interleave the quilt with a sheet of bubblewrap, acid-free tissue paper, or both. Don't use colored tissue paper because the colors run. Rolling from the top down means the top edge will be in the smallest part of the roll but will have the full weight of the quilt to pull any curve out when it is hung. Wrap the completed quilt in more packaging.

398
Delivery services

Before you pack the quilt, you need to know how it will be delivered. This information usually has to be included on the entry form but it is sometimes possible to change from postal or courier delivery to personal delivery.
• **In person** Quilts that need to be posted have to be sent in advance of the exhibition whereas delivery in person can sometimes be made to the exhibition venue a few days in advance. Personal delivery allows extra time to finish your quilt, fewer restrictions over packaging sizes and being able to keep your packaging materials. Often one member of a quilt group will volunteer to deliver several quilts in person. You will be given a receipt for each quilt that you will need when collecting.
• **By mail** If you are sending your quilt long distance, personal delivery isn't an option, so check out carriers and postage services to determine which will be best for you. Quilts have been lost in transit, so check the insurance and compensation levels carefully. There are maximum package sizes and weights too. For international shows, use a shipping company that can deal with the customs forms for you. The quilt will be a temporary importation, as it will be returning to its country of origin. It has been known for customs duty problems to arise when quilts are returned if the correct paperwork isn't completed.

399
Dealing with large quilts

Larger quilts are long when rolled, so folding the quilt into a box may be the only option. Fold the quilt horizontally first, then vertically, packing the folds with scrunched up acid-free tissue paper to minimize creases. Making a loose, flattened roll is another method, with the front of the quilt on the outside, then making vertical folds packed with tissue paper. Ensure the box is large enough so your quilt isn't crushed.

Exhibition organizers don't usually have space to store specialized packaging materials, so check how your quilt will be returned. A long calico drawstring bag, made to measure for a rolled quilt, is great if you are delivering personally and can bring the packaging away with you.

400
Collecting the quilt

Keep the receipt safe. You will need it, and possibly some extra identification, to collect the quilt at the end of a show. The quilts will be taken down, loosely bagged up, and take to a collection point. Allow enough time at the end of the show for the quilts to be taken off the display before going to the collection point. There may be space for you to repackage your quilt. Quilts that are not collected personally will be returned by post or courier, depending on the service selected on the entry form.

Care and storage

Having spent time and effort making your quilts, it makes sense to look after them, so you can enjoy them for a long time and perhaps hand them on to future generations as family heirlooms.

"Stars Sampler"
by Dot Sherlock
Keeping decoration neutral can show a bold quilt to its best advantage. Adapted from "Houston Stars" by Gwenfai Rees Griffiths.

401

Quilt storage

Store quilts flat if possible. Bed quilts can be stacked flat on a guest bed and covered with a sheet, although they will have to be moved every time you have a guest. If you have to fold quilts for storage, pad the folds with rolls of acid-free tissue paper. Wrap the folded quilt in a cotton sheet or pillowcase. Do not wrap quilts in plastic, which can trap moisture, and never wrap a quilt in an opaque trash bag for any reason—more than one quilt has been lost to the garbage collection by mistake.

Quilts should be taken out of storage and refolded with the folds in a different place every few months to prevent creases developing. Make sure your storage area is dry, away from direct sunlight, and free from bugs and moths. Attics and cellars are not good places to store quilts, as extreme fluctuations in temperature are not good for textiles.

"Dancing colors"
Quilts look just as good in modern minimalist rooms as in more traditional interiors. The wallhanging below was designed to reduce echo in a room without many other soft furnishings, as well as to decorate the space. It is hung from a wooden lath, fixed invisibly to the wall with mirror plates.

402

Use and display

• Sunlight is an enemy of quilts—it fades the fabrics and accelerates aging. Blinds and shades will help screen the sun, as above right. Constant exposure to strong sunlight in conservatories and sunrooms fades a quilt very quickly, so if you want to use a quilt in a brightly lit room, use cream or white and don't leave the quilt out when not in use.
• Quilts displayed on beds or draped over sofas are also exposed to light. Turn quilts frequently to even out any fading. Try displaying quilts in rotation.
• Locate wallhangings out of direct sunlight or change them from time to time. Larger wallhangings are heavy, so take them down and lay them flat to rest them, taking the stress off the patchwork seams. Wallhangings with embellishments are also quite heavy, so rest these from time to time as well.

403

Care of vintage quilts

Avoid washing antique and
vintage quilts (right) unless
absolutely necessary. Dust and
loose dirt may be vacuumed
away, covering the quilt
with a layer of net first.
Hold the vacuum-cleaning
nozzle above the quilt
so the material cannot
get sucked up and use
a low power setting, if
possible. If the quilt
must be washed,
handwash it but do
not machine spin.
If you are in any
doubt, consult
a textile
conservator first.

404

Cleaning quilts

Quilts that are in regular use will need cleaning from time to time. Consider the
fabrics used, the batting, and any embellishments before cleaning. If you have used
washable materials throughout and have prewashed the fabrics and batting (see
pages 20 and 105), you should be able to wash the quilt without problems. Dry-
cleaning is a possibility but you will need to know exactly what fibers are in the
quilt and trust your dry-cleaner.
• **Machine wash** Quilts made with new, prewashed cotton fabrics and with modern
cotton or polyester batting can be machine-washed. Use a mild detergent designed
for delicate fibers or soapflakes rather than stronger detergents, and avoid any with
optical brighteners, which will seem to fade your quilt. Use a cool wash setting
for delicate items. The quilt can be tumble-dried on a medium setting or dried flat
on towels covered with a sheet, covered with another sheet if you are doing this
outside. Wet or damp quilts should not be hung on a clothesline, as the extra
weight of water will put a lot of strain on the stitching. If you have a large or thick
quilt that would be a tight squeeze in a domestic washing machine, use the larger
machines at a launderette.
• **Hand wash** Quilts can be washed by hand in the bathtub, by kneading the quilt
gently in warm water with soapflakes. Rinse the quilt thoroughly several times,
allowing the water to drain out of the bath each time. Once the water runs clear,
drain the bath and gently squeeze as much water out of the quilt as you can. Use a
large towel to support the quilt and take it out of the bath. Spread the quilt out to
dry as above. The quilt will be heavy with water when removed from the bath, so
put it through a washing-machine spin-cycle, unless it is fragile.

FIX IT

405 Hanging out

Quilt hanging options include
fancy hangers made specially for
quilts, like the wire hanger below.
If you plan to use a special quilt
hanger that is non-adjustable, it
is easier to make your quilt to fit
the hanger, rather than trying to
find a hanger to fit the quilt.

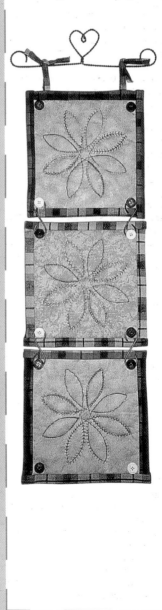

Estimating fabric quantities and math reference

Math for quilting isn't difficult. Use these basic tips as a quick reference when designing and planning your quilt.

Calculating fabric quantities

For a rough idea of how much fabric you need, note down how many blocks you want to make, then the sizes and number of pieces for each fabric. Multiply these together. For example, if you need four 2½ in (6.4 cm) squares for each block and there are 20 blocks, you will need 80 squares. To cut these in four rows of 20 squares across 42-in (105-cm) wide fabric would require 15 in (38.1 cm) of fabric, allowing 15 squares in each row. Add a little extra in case the fabric is cut slightly off the grain and remember you cannot use the selvedges. If the fabric is "fussy cut," selecting a particular motif or stripe direction, you will need more fabric.

Basic patch sizes

These diagrams are a handy quick reference for working out the cutting sizes for half- and quarter-square triangles, 45-degree diamonds, and trapezoids.

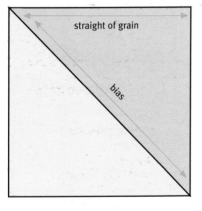

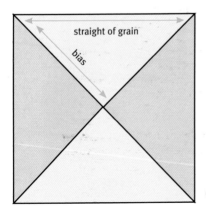

Subcutting square into half-square triangles
Add ⅞ in (2.2 cm) to finished size of the square.

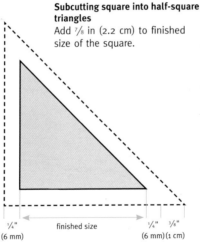

Subcutting square into quarter-square triangles
Add 1¼ in (3.2 cm) to finished size of the square.

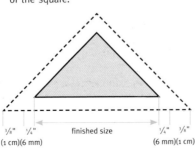

Subcutting strip into 45-degree diamonds
The width of the strip (a) equals the width between the parallel sides (b). The seam allowance around the shape is ¼ in (6 mm).

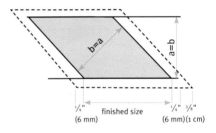

Subcutting 45-degree miters
The width of the strip equals the width between the parallel sides.

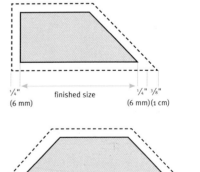

Subcutting 45-degree trapezoids
The width of the strip equals the width between the parallel sides.

Imperial/metric conversions

Multiply sizes in inches by 2.54 and round up or down to the nearest millimeter, for example 4 in = 10.2 cm

Divide centimeters by 2.54 for imperial measurements.

inches	centimeters
1	2.5
1 1/8	2.9
1 1/4	3.2
1 3/8	3.5
1 1/2	3.8
1 5/8	4.1
1 3/4	4.4
1 7/8	4.8
2	5
2 1/8	5.4
2 1/4	5.7
2 3/8	6
2 1/2	6.4
2 5/8	6.7
2 3/4	7
2 7/8	7.3
3	7.6
3 1/8	7.9
3 1/4	8.3
3 3/8	8.6
3 1/2	8.9
3 5/8	9.2
3 3/4	9.5
3 7/8	9.8
4	10.2
4 1/8	10.5
4 1/4	10.8
4 3/8	11.1
4 1/2	11.4
4 5/8	11.7
4 3/4	12
4 7/8	12.4
5	12.7
5 1/8	13
5 1/4	13.3
5 3/8	13.7
5 1/2	14
5 5/8	14.3
5 3/4	14.6
5 7/8	14.9
6	15.2
6 1/8	15.6
6 1/4	15.9
6 3/8	16.2
6 1/2	16.5
6 5/8	16.8
6 3/4	17.1
6 7/8	17.5
7	17.8
7 1/8	18.1
7 1/4	18.4
7 3/8	18.7
7 1/2	19
7 5/8	19.4
7 3/4	19.7
7 7/8	20
8	20.3
8 1/8	20.6
8 1/4	21
8 3/8	21.3
8 1/2	21.6
8 5/8	21.9
8 3/4	22.2
8 7/8	22.5
9	22.9
9 1/8	23.2
9 1/4	23.5
9 3/8	23.8
9 1/2	24

Useful addresses

Clotilde
P.O. Box 7500
Big Sandy, TX 75755-7500
Tel: 1-800-545-4002
E-mail: customer_service@ clotilde.com
www.clotilde.com
Fabrics and quilting supplies

Connecting Threads
13118 NE 4th Street
Vancouver, WA 98684
Tel: 360-260-8900
E-mail: customerservice@ connectingthreads.com
www.connectingthreads.com
Fabrics and quilting supplies

eQuilter.com
5455 Spine Road
Suite E
Boulder, CO 80301
Tel: Toll free 877-FABRIC-3; or 303-527-0856
E-mail: service@equilter.com
www.eQuilter.com
Fabrics and quilting supplies

Fabric Depot
700 SE 122nd Avenue
Portland, OR 97233
Tel: 503-252-9530
E-mail: info@fabricdepot.com
www.fabricdepot.com
Fabrics and quilting supplies

Fat Quarter Shop
P.O. Box 1544
Manchaca, TX 78652
Tel: toll free 866-826-2069; or 512-292-9717
E-mail: Kimberly@FatQuarterShop.com
www.fatquartershop.com
Best for fat quarters

Hancocks of Paducah
3841 Hinkleville Rd
Paducah, KY 42001
Tel: Toll free 1-800-845-8723; or 270-443-4410
E-mail: customerservice@hancocks-paducah.com
www.hancocks-paducah.com
Fabrics and quilting supplies

Jo-Ann
5555 Darrow Road
Hudson, OH 44236
Tel: 1-888-739-4120
www.joann.com
Fabrics and quilting supplies

Keepsake Quilting
P.O. Box 1618
Center Harbor, NH 03226
Tel: 1-800-525-8086
E-mail: customerservice@ keepsakequilting.com
www.keepsakequilting.com
Fabrics and quilting supplies

Purl Soho
147 Sullivan Street
New York, NY 10012
Tel: 212-420-8798
www.purlsoho.com
Fabrics and quilting supplies

ReproductionFabrics.com
205 Haggerty Lane, Suite 190
Bozeman, MT 59715
Tel: 406-586-1775
E-mail: staff@reproductionfabrics.com
www.reproductionfabrics.com
True document reproduction fabrics

Shibori Dragon
1124 Gravelly Lake Drive SW
Lakewood, WA 98499
Tel: 253-582-7455
E-mail: shiboridragon@juno.com
www.shiboridragon.com
Japanese textiles and sashiko supplies

The City Quilter
133 West 25th Street
New York, NY 10001
Tel: 212-807-0390
E-mail: info@cityquilter.com
www.cityquilter.com
Fabrics and quilting supplies, including Japanese

Contact the author through her website at www.susanbriscoe.co.uk

Glossary

American patchwork
Seamed patchwork sewn with hand running stitch or by machine.

Appliqué
Individual shapes sewn to a background fabric.

Backing
The bottom layer of the quilt, under the top and batting.

Backing fabric
Any fabric used for the back of the quilt.

Bagging out
Turning an item right side out after it has been sewn with right sides together, e.g. a cushion. Also used for invisible-edge finish.

Balance marks
Points marked on adjacent patches to be matched when stitching curves. Also known as "notches."

Basting
Large running stitches used to hold two or more layers in position before final sewing or quilting.

Batik
Wax-resist dyed fabrics, often hand dyed.

Batting
The layer placed between the quilt top and the backing, for warmth and appearance.

Bed quilt
A large quilt made to cover the top (and sometimes sides) of a bed, to be viewed laying flat.

Bias strip appliqué
Used to make narrow designs such as flower stems.

Big stitch
Hand quilting with larger running stitches and thicker threads.

Binding
A method of finishing raw edges around the sides of the quilt by enclosing them in strips of folded fabric.

Block
Unit of patchwork made from several pieces. May be repeated or used alone.

Blocking
Easing the finished quilt to lie square and flat, usually by dampening and drying the quilt.

Broderie persé
Printed motifs cut out from fabric and used as appliqué pieces.

Butting
A method of finishing edges by turning them in toward each other.

Chain piecing
Machine sewing patchwork pieces together without cutting the thread between sewn pieces.

Cheater panel
Fabric printed with a large, ready-to-use design, sometimes faux patchwork.

Compass
Mathematical instrument for drawing curves and circles.

Contour quilting
Quilting lines parallel to patchwork seams.

Corded quilting
Designs made by threading cord or thick yarn between parallel lines of stitching.

Counterchange
Reversing colors on a pattern to emphasize negative and positive shapes.

Coverlet
Patchwork bedcover with backing but no batting.

Crazy patchwork
Patchwork made from randomly shaped pieces, usually appliquéd. May include lace, ribbon, embellishments, etc.

Cross hatching
Quilting in a grid pattern, regular or variable.

Darning foot
A sewing machine foot used when the machine feed is disengaged for free-motion quilting.

Directional print
Fabric with motifs in one direction, sometimes in stripes, with an obvious right way up.

Echo quilting
Quilting a series of parallel lines following the outline of a shape, often used for appliqué.

Embellishment
Anything that can be sewn decoratively to the quilt front.

Embroidery foot
See *Darning foot*.

English patchwork
A method of making patchwork by basting fabric over papers, then whipstitching the seams by hand (also called English paper piecing).

Facing
A finishing method which adds extra fabric to the back of the quilt edges, allowing piping, Prairie Points, and other inserted edges.

Fat quarter
A yard (or meter) of fabric quartered equally by cutting down and across.

Faux binding
A finishing method with the backing wrapped to the front, without extra binding strips added.

Five-patch
Patchwork blocks on a 5 x 5 grid.

Foiling
Decorating fabric with metallic accents from sheet foil.

Foundation piecing
A method of making patchwork sewn to a fabric (permanent) or paper (temporary) backing (the "foundation").

Four-patch
Patchwork block with four main units.

Free motion foot
See *Darning foot*.

Freezer paper
Thick white paper that can be ironed onto fabric as a temporary stitching guide. Useful for appliqué.

Fusible webbing
Paper with adhesive web on one side; used for appliqué.

Fused appliqué
Individual appliqué shapes ironed onto the background before stitching.

Fussy cutting
Patchwork pieces cut selectively from a printed fabric.

Geometric
Mathematical proportioning of shapes, lines, angles, points, surfaces, and solids.

Grid
A pattern of horizontal and vertical lines.

Half-square triangle
Patchwork square made of two equal triangles (also called "triangle square").

Hanging sleeve
A tube of fabric sewn to the top back of a quilt, as a means of hanging it up.

Hawaiian appliqué
Traditional symmetrical, linked appliqué motifs, usually large, created like folded paper cuts.

In the ditch
Quilting patchwork along the seam line.

Isometric grid
A grid based on 60-degree triangles. Hexagons, six-pointed stars, and other patterns based on that angle are drafted on this type of grid.

Interlacing
The appearance of strands going under and over each other, as in weaving.

Japanese folded patchwork
Modern technique to make individually finished units, folding the backing fabric to the front.

Kantha
Traditional quilting from Bangladesh, usually in colors on white.

Lapped binding
Quilt edging with squared-off overlaps at the corners.

Log Cabin
Patchwork blocks made of strips, assembled outward from a center (or corner) square.

Long-arm machine
An industrial sewing machine with a wide area under the machine throat, used for professional machine quilting.

Machine trapunto
Extra pieces of batting inserted into a quilting design for 3D effect.

Medallion quilt
Patchwork design with a sequence of sections and borders around a central panel.

Mini print
Small-scale printed cotton.

Mitered binding
Quilt edging with corners resembling picture frames.

Mitering
Technique for finishing quilt borders to resemble picture frames.

Mosaic patchwork
Alternative name for English patchwork, reflecting the complex patterns, resembling mosaic floor-tiles, that can be pieced by this method.

Muslin—plain
Woven, natural-colored cotton. Sold in varying qualities, from fine to heavyweight.

Needleturn appliqué
The point of the sewing needle is used to turn under a narrow hem around the appliqué shape.

Neutrals
White, black, or gray fabrics.

Nine-patch
Patchwork block with nine main units.

Ombre
A shaded effect.

Posts
Square patches set where sashing strips meet.

Prairie point
Folded fabric triangles used as edges and insertions.

Quarter-square triangle
Patchwork square made of four equal triangles.

Quilt-as-you-go
Quilting the quilt in smaller sections before assembly.

Quilt sandwich
The backing, batting, and top quilt layers—the batting is the "sandwich filling."

Quilter's rule (or ruler)
Ruler marked with parallel grids for rotary cutting. May be imperial (inches) or metric (centimeters).

Reverse appliqué
A hole is cut from the background fabric and the appliqué fabric added from behind but sewn from the front.

Rotary cutter
A cutting tool with a disc blade.

Round-robin
A quilt made by several different quilters taking turns, usually as one of a set of quilts.

Sashiko
Japanese stitching, usually in white on blue.

Sashing
Fabric strips set between quilt blocks, usually of a contrasting color.

Sawtooth triangles
Folded fabric triangles used as edges and insertions. May be interlocked.

Scrap quilt
Patchwork with a large selection of fabrics, often over 70 in one quilt.

Seminole patchwork
Patchwork made by cutting and rearranging units from pieced strips.

Set
The layout of blocks in a quilt.

Seven-patch
Patchwork blocks on a 7 x 7 grid.

Shadow appliqué
Appliqué with a layer of translucent fabric on top.

Shot cotton
Fabric woven with two contrasting thread colors.

String patchwork
Patchwork made from narrow strips.

Strippy quilt
Quilt designed in columns.

Template
A paper, cardboard, or plastic piece used to cut out a patchwork, quilting, or appliqué shape.

Thin quarter
A yard (or meter) of fabric cut into four equal pieces across the width, at right angles to the selvedge.

Tone-on-tone
Fabric printed in tones of the same color.

Trapunto
Traditional Italian stuffed quilting.

Turned-in edges
A traditional finishing method without additional binding.

Tying
Individual knots used to hold the quilt sandwich together.

Wallhanging
A quilt designed to be used as a picture and viewed vertically.

Walking foot
A sewing machine foot that helps to feed several fabric layers through the machine at the same rate.

Wholecloth
Traditional quilt made without patchwork.

Wrapped edge
See *Faux binding*.

Yo-yos
Gathered fabric circles used for embellishment or sewn edge to edge.

Index

Fold out this flap

Use the information below to calculate bed quilt sizes.

Standard bed and quilt sizes

Batting sizes

craft	45 x 36 in (114 x 91 cm)
crib	60 x 45 in (152 x 114 cm)
twin	92 x 72 in (234 x 183 cm)
queen	92 x 108 in (234 x 274 cm)
king	120 x 120 in (305 x 305 cm)

Standard bed mattress sizes (may vary)

crib	46 x 23 in (117 x 58 cm)
twin	75 x 39 in (190 x 99 cm)
full/double	75 x 54 in (190 x 137 cm)
queen	80 x 60 in (203 x 152 cm)
king	80 x 76 in (203 x 193 cm)

Remember:

The quilt center usually corresponds to the mattress size.

Add 12 in (31 cm) to the length of the center panel (= mattress size) to tuck under pillows, if desired.

Measure the height of the bed, e.g., 18 in (46 cm) and add this measurement to three sides only.

Bed quilt borders may be on four sides or on three sides only.

Credits

I would like to thank the following quilters for allowing me to feature their work—Diane Abram, Linda Bilsborrow, Rebecca Collins, Betty Coops, Catherine Falmer, Ferret, Deborah Gordon, Gwenfai Rees Griffiths, Lilian Hedley, Jenny Hewer, Kathy Home, Barbara Howell, Jean Jackson, Jennifer Lewis, Jane Mariott, Pat Morris, Sheena Norquay, Linda Paris (sample on page 114), Maureen Poole, Bethany Reynolds (*Magic Stack-n-Whack Quilts*), Dot Sherlock, Pat Storey (*Geometrical Quilts*), Nikki Tinkler, Charlotte Turner, Gill Young, and members of Alsager Ps & Qs, the Tuesday Strippers, Gresford Craft Group and Wrexham Quilting Circle. Many thanks to Maureen Poole and Bridgid Ockleton for permission to use photos of their antique quilts. The kantha sample on page 119 is included by kind permission of Nikki Tinkler (*The Quilter's Stitch Bible*) and the foiling sample on page 25 is by Sally Holman (*The Quilter's Directory of Embellishments*). Thanks to my family and friends for their support (including my cats, Fluff and Takenoko, who appears on page 111), to Yasuko Okazaki and the staff at Clover, Japan, to our photographers for creating beautiful images, and to the great team at Quarto for producing another lovely book!

All uncredited quilts are by the author.

For Mum & Dad

Quarto would also like to thank the following agencies:
p21b, 23 Shutterstock
p44, 45bl Corbis
b = bottom; l = left

All other photographs and illustrations are the copyright of Quarto Publishing plc. While every effort has been made to credit contributors, Quarto would like to apologize should there have been any omissions or errors—and would be pleased to make the appropriate correction for future editions of the book.